Alternative Diets

Series Editor: Cara Acred

Volume 288

0069062X

Independence Educational Publishers

First published by Independence Educational Publishers

The Studio, High Green

Great Shelford

Cambridge CB22 5EG

England

© Independence 2015

British Library Cataloguing in Publication Data

Alternative diets. -- (Issues ; 288)
1. Vegetarianism. 2. Veganism. 3. Animal welfare--Moral
and ethical aspects.
I. Series II. Acred, Cara editor.
179.3-dc23

ISBN-13: 9781861687203

Printed in Great Britain
Zenith Print Group

Contents

Introduction

Alternative Diets is Volume 288 in the **ISSUES** series. The aim of the series is to offer current, diverse information about important issues in our world, from a UK perspective.

ABOUT ALTERNATIVE DIETS

One of the biggest issues facing our society is the challenge of achieving a healthy diet that is sustainable, but also provides us with optimum nutrition. Many people in the UK, and globally, believe that 'flexitarianism' is the answer – eating less meat and more vegetables. Some believe that going gluten-free is the solution, although others are sceptical of what could be classed as a fad with no real health benefits. This book explores alternative diets, considering the implications for those with chronic illnesses, the sustainability of meat-free diets and more.

OUR SOURCES

Titles in the **ISSUES** series are designed to function as educational resource books, providing a balanced overview of a specific subject.

The information in our books is comprised of facts, articles and opinions from many different sources, including:

⇨ Newspaper reports and opinion pieces

⇨ Website factsheets

⇨ Magazine and journal articles

⇨ Statistics and surveys

⇨ Government reports

⇨ Literature from special interest groups

A NOTE ON CRITICAL EVALUATION

Because the information reprinted here is from a number of different sources, readers should bear in mind the origin of the text and whether the source is likely to have a particular bias when presenting information (or when conducting their research). It is hoped that, as you read about the many aspects of the issues explored in this book, you will critically evaluate the information presented.

It is important that you decide whether you are being presented with facts or opinions. Does the writer give a biased or unbiased report? If an opinion is being expressed, do you agree with the writer? Is there potential bias to the 'facts' or statistics behind an article?

ASSIGNMENTS

In the back of this book, you will find a selection of assignments designed to help you engage with the articles you have been reading and to explore your own opinions. Some tasks will take longer than others and there is a mixture of design, writing and research-based activities that you can complete alone or in a group.

FURTHER RESEARCH

At the end of each article we have listed its source and a website that you can visit if you would like to conduct your own research. Please remember to critically evaluate any sources that you consult and consider whether the information you are viewing is accurate and unbiased.

Useful weblinks

www.animalaid.org.uk

www.bda.uk.com

www.theconversation.com

www.foeeurope.org

www.futureoffood.ox.ac.uk

www.theguardian.com

www.huffingtonpost.co.uk/jon-young/

www.imperial.ac.uk

www.independent.co.uk

www.mintel.com

www.naturalbalancefoods.co.uk

www.nhs.uk

www.nutrition.org.uk

www.oxfordmartin.ox.ac.uk

blog.practicalethics.ox.ac.uk

www.telegraph.co.uk

Healthy, sustainable diets – what are the issues?

How can we achieve a dietary pattern that provides us with the many nutrients we need for health, in appropriate amounts, but that is also equitable, affordable and sustainable? And, how do we produce more food with fewer resources, such as land, water and fuel, to feed the growing global population?

These are some of the key questions that we face in the 21st century and which we need to find answers to, and quickly. The British Nutrition Foundation and many others from government, farming, food industry, academia and other sectors are working together on this important issue. The aim is to find solutions to these challenges that are evidence-based, realistic and will achieve the required impact both in the UK and globally.

This is an emerging area and we do not have all the answers yet. Though what we do know is that we need to start taking action now to secure a sustainable global food supply for future generations, and that all sectors of society have a role to play.

There are currently huge pressures on the global food system. The demand for food is increasing with the growing global population (which is expected to increase from seven billion today to over nine billion by 2050) and also with the increase in wealth in emerging economies, as this creates demand for a more varied, high-quality diet (i.e. typically more meat and dairy foods). To simply produce more food using current production methods and technologies to meet this increased demand is unsustainable, as this would require more land, more water and more energy, which are finite resources. At the same time, climate change is occurring and will become increasingly apparent unless we take action now.

According to the World Wildlife Fund (WWF), we are already consuming natural resources at a faster rate than the planet's capacity to replenish them. The WWF calculates that if the world's population consumed natural resources at the rate of the UK we would need three planets to support us, clearly illustrating that things need to change.

A recent government report by Foresight (2011) titled *The Future of Food and Farming: challenges and choices for global sustainability* defined sustainable/sustainability as:

'A system or state where the needs of the present and local population can be met without diminishing the ability of future generations or populations in other locations to meet their needs and without causing harm to the environment and natural assets.'

Defining a 'sustainable diet' is a complex issue and there are many factors to consider. As well as environmental, social and economic factors, a key factor is that food is a basic need. A healthy, varied diet provides us with the energy and nutrients we need for health, normal body function and physical activity.

This emphasises the need for health and sustainability agendas to be considered in tandem, in order to achieve a sustainable and secure food supply for future generations that also supports public health.

Food not only provides us with the fuel and nutrients to sustain life but is a big part of many cultures and plays a significant role socially.

In the UK, most of us are fortunate enough to eat what we like, when we like. In today's global food market, we have come to expect to buy most foods all year round, such as leeks in summer and strawberries at Christmas time. Most of us eat regularly throughout the day, often without giving much thought to where the food has come from or how it was produced. But looking ahead, we will need to change our food consumption patterns.

The need to change what we choose to eat is further highlighted when we consider the global health challenges that we face, specifically that:

⇨ Over one billion people worldwide are overweight or obese;

⇨ One billion others do not have access to adequate food; and

⇨ An additional one billion have inadequate micronutrient intakes.

Ending hunger is one of the key challenges to address at a global level. This goes beyond simply producing enough food in the world so that everyone can potentially be fed, as this food needs to be accessible and affordable by all.

In the UK, we see evidence of both over- and under-consumption of dietary energy and nutrients – despite

Facts & figures

Did you know...

1. The global population will increase from nearly seven billion today to eight billion by 2030, and to probably over nine billion by 2050. Historically the global population growth rate was very low and prior to the industrial revolution (from the 18th to the 19th century) the world's population was less than one billion people.

2. The global food system currently uses 70% of the extracted fresh water and 34.3% of the land area, and is a major producer of greenhouse gas (GHG) emissions.

3. Globally, agriculture (including fertiliser production) directly contributes ten to 12% of GHG emissions. This figure rises to 30% or more when land conversion and costs beyond the farm gate are added.

4. In the UK, GHG emissions associated with agriculture are lower than the global average at approximately 7%, as are total GHG emissions associated with the food supply chain (i.e. production and consumption) at approximately 18%.

5. Globally, agriculture contributes a disproportionate amount of high impact GHGs (e.g. methane and nitrous oxide).

6. Low- and middle-income countries (e.g. India, Kenya, Bangladesh and Colombia) are currently responsible for about three quarters of agricultural GHG emissions (with land use change included) and their proportionate share is increasing (especially in Africa and Latin America).

7. UK farming and fishing account for about one third of GHG emissions from the food supply chain (approximately 7% of the total). The majority of GHG emissions are due to emissions from ruminant animals (i.e. cows and sheep) and the oxidisation of nitrogen in fertilisers.

8. Net trade and commercial transportation contribute 25% and 9% respectively of the GHG emissions in the UK food chain (net trade covers emissions related to the production of food imports and exports, but not transportation).

Source: Foresight (2011) The Future of Food and Farming:
Challenges and choices for global sustainability. *Government Office for Science.*

more than 60% of adults currently classified as overweight or obese, many people still have inadequate intakes of some micronutrients due to poor dietary choices.

Overall, we need diets that are both healthy and sustainable. This creates the opportunity for environmental and other sustainability messages to be tagged onto current messages about healthy eating. But what is a healthy, sustainable diet?

The FAO (Food and Agricultural Organization of the United Nations) defines 'sustainable diets' as:

'Those diets with low environmental impacts which contribute to food and nutrition security and to healthy life for present and future generations. Sustainable diets are protective and respectful of biodiversity and ecosystems, culturally acceptable, accessible, economically fair and affordable; nutritionally adequate, safe and healthy; while optimising natural and human resources.'

By changing our diets – the types of foods we eat and how often we eat certain foods – there is potential to ease the pressures on the global food system.

However, exactly which changes we should make to ensure that we have a healthy and sustainable diet are not yet known. As yet there is no simple set of principles that we as consumers can apply, in all cases, to identify foods that are more sustainable than others.

However, there is enough evidence to support specific actions now in the UK with regards to: following the Eatwell plate dietary pattern, choosing fish from sustainable stocks and reducing food waste in the home.

1. Adopt the Eatwell plate dietary pattern

The Eatwell plate is designed to help all those aged over two years of age to eat a healthy, balanced diet as it shows how much of what is eaten should come from each food group.

The Eatwell plate model has been promoted in the UK for many years, though most of us still eat too much saturated fat, sugar and salt, too little fibre, and too few fruits and vegetables.

As well as improving health, there is growing evidence that following the Eatwell dietary pattern will also help reduce greenhouse gas emissions associated with food production. Also, it is generally accepted that sustainable dietary patterns for the future can justifiably include a variety of both plant and animal foods to support health and promote biodiversity. This is particularly important as different foods contain different nutrients, and therefore we need to eat a variety of foods to obtain sufficient amounts of the many nutrients we need for health.

The Eatwell model shows that we should eat some foods from each of the main four food groups every day, with more of some foods than others. Our diets should be based on starchy carbohydrate foods (e.g. bread, potatoes, rice and pasta), as well as plenty of fruits and vegetables. A variety of foods from these two food groups should make up two-thirds of the food we eat. Most of the remaining third of the diet should be made up of milk and dairy foods, meat, fish, eggs, beans and other non-dairy sources of protein. Foods in the fifth group (foods and drinks high in fat and/or sugar) (e.g. cakes, chocolate, sweets, biscuits, fizzy drinks, crisps) can also be included sparingly in our diets for palatability.

2. Eat fish regularly but choose wisely

In the UK, current dietary guidelines recommend that adults eat two portions of fish a week, one of which should be an oily species (e.g. salmon, mackerel, fresh tuna). Fish is a good source of protein and contains many vitamins and minerals, and oily fish is also high in omega-3 fatty acids, which are not found in many foods and are beneficial for heart health.

It is a fact that overfishing of some of the world's oceans has lead to limited stocks of some species in certain zones. It is this discovery that has raised concerns about the appropriateness of the dietary advice to eat more fish. However, experts believe that with good fisheries management, the decline will be reversed.

As consumers of fish, we can also do our bit to help replenish these limited fish stocks:

⇨ Choose as wide a variety of species as possible.

⇨ Try experimenting with less familiar species for which stocks are believed to be more abundant, such as coley, gurnard and mackerel.

⇨ Look out for ecolabels on certified fish products at the supermarket, such as the blue Marine Stewardship Council logo.

3. Reduce household food waste

It is estimated that UK households waste 8.3 million tonnes of food every year, costing them £12 billion and contributing 3% of UK greenhouse gas emissions.

The problem with food waste from a sustainability perspective relates to the precious resources that are used in the production of the food (i.e. water, land and energy) and also the carbon emissions associated with its disposal.

We can follow these simple tips to reduce food waste in the home:

⇨ Avoid cooking more food than is required.

⇨ Plan meals before going to the shops and only buy what is needed.

⇨ Use foods before they reach their 'use-by' date. Keep an eye on foods with a 'best-before' date and try to eat these foods before this date to ensure that the quality is still high.

⇨ Find creative ways to use leftovers.

⇨ Follow the storage instructions on food labels.

For more details on how to reduce household food waste, visit the Love Food Hate Waste campaign website (www.lovefoodhatewaste.com).

⇨ The above information is reprinted with kind permission from the British Nutrition Foundation. Please visit www.nutrition.org.uk for further information. **WQEIC LRC**

Vegetarian and vegan diets Q&A

Read our answers to common questions about staying healthy on a vegetarian or vegan diet, from looking after your bones to healthy eating in pregnancy.

What is a vegetarian?

Vegetarians and vegans don't eat any meat, poultry, game, fish, shellfish or crustacea (such as crab or lobster), or animal by-products (such as gelatine).

Vegetarians eat a diet of grains, pulses, nuts, seeds, fruit and vegetables, dairy products and eggs. Vegetarians who also don't eat eggs and dairy products are called vegans.

There are three main types of vegetarian:

⇨ Lacto-ovo-vegetarians eat both dairy products and eggs. This is the most common type of vegetarian diet.

⇨ Lacto-vegetarians eat dairy products but not eggs.

⇨ Vegans do not eat dairy products, eggs, or any other animal product.

At what age is it safe to become a vegetarian or vegan?

As long as they get all the nutrients they need, children can be brought up healthily on a vegetarian or vegan diet.

Children need plenty of energy and protein to help them grow and develop. It's also important that vegetarian and vegan children get

enough iron, calcium, vitamin B12 and vitamin D.

If you're bringing up your child on a diet without meat or fish (vegetarian) or without any food from animals (vegan), they will need two or three portions of vegetable protein or nuts every day to give them enough protein and iron. Don't give whole nuts to children under five as they could choke. Grind the nuts finely or use a smooth nut butter.

It is recommended that all children aged six months to five years old are given supplements containing vitamins A, C and D unless they drink more than 500ml (about a pint) of infant formula a day.

Vitamin drops are especially important for vegetarian and vegan children between six months and five years old. They may also need a vitamin B12 supplement. If your child is older than this, speak to your GP or a dietitian to see whether vitamin supplements should be included in their diet.

Can babies and children have a vegan diet?

If you're breastfeeding and you're on a vegan diet, it's especially important for you to take a vitamin D supplement. You may also need extra vitamin B12.

Take care when feeding children on a vegan diet. Young children need a good variety of foods to provide the energy and vitamins they need for growth.

A vegan diet can be bulky and high in fibre. This can mean that children get full up before they've eaten enough calories and nutrients. Because of this, they may need extra supplements. Ask a dietitian or doctor for advice before you start introducing your child to solids.

Is it safe to be a vegetarian or vegan during pregnancy?

A varied and balanced vegetarian or vegan diet can provide enough nutrients for you and your baby during pregnancy. However, you might find it hard to get enough iron, vitamin D and vitamin B12.

Talk to your doctor or midwife about how to get enough of these important nutrients. All pregnant and breastfeeding women are advised to take a vitamin D supplement, regardless of their diet.

What are the health benefits of a vegetarian diet?

A vegetarian diet can be very healthy, but your diet won't automatically be healthier if you cut out meat. Like everyone, vegetarians need to make sure they eat a balanced diet containing:

⇨ plenty of fruit and vegetables (at least five portions of a variety of fruit and vegetables a day)

⇨ plenty of potatoes, bread, rice, pasta and other starchy foods (choosing brown or wholegrain varieties where possible)

⇨ some milk and dairy foods

⇨ some eggs, beans and other non-dairy sources of protein

⇨ just a small amount of foods and drinks high in fat and sugar.

Do vegetarians and vegans need vitamin supplements?

With good planning and an understanding of what makes up a healthy balanced vegetarian and vegan diet, you can get all the nutrients your body needs to be healthy without the need for supplements.

However, if your diet is not planned properly, you could miss out on essential nutrients. Vegetarians need to make sure they get enough iron and vitamin B12, and vegans enough calcium, iron and vitamin B12. Women are thought to be at particular risk of iron deficiency, including those on a vegetarian or vegan diet.

How can I get enough iron?

Although meat is the best source of iron, other good sources of iron include:

⇨ pulses, such as beans, lentils and peas

⇨ nuts

⇨ dried fruit, such as raisins

⇨ dark-green vegetables, such as watercress, broccoli and spring greens

⇨ wholegrains, such as brown rice and brown bread

⇨ cereals fortified with iron.

The amount of iron adults need is about 8.7mg a day for men and about 14.8mg a day for women. As long as you remember to regularly include the above foods in your diet, you should be getting enough iron.

How can I get enough calcium?

Calcium helps maintain strong bones. Non-vegans get most of their calcium from dairy foods, so it's important for vegans to get calcium from other foods.

Good sources of calcium for vegans are:

⇨ fortified soya, rice and oat milk

⇨ leafy green vegetables (but not spinach)

⇨ almonds

⇨ sesame seeds and tahini

⇨ dried fruit

⇨ pulses

⇨ brown (wholemeal) and white bread.

Adults need about 700mg of calcium a day, so it's important that vegans regularly include plenty of these foods in their diet.

The body needs vitamin D to absorb calcium. Fortified margarine and fat spreads, fortified breakfast cereals and egg yolks contain vitamin D. The body also makes its own vitamin D when exposed to sunshine. Bones get stronger when you use them and the best way to do this is through regular exercise.

How can I get enough vitamin B12?

Vitamin B12 is only found naturally in foods from animal sources, so sources for vegans are limited and a vitamin B12 supplement may be needed. If you eat dairy products and eggs, you probably get enough.

Vegan sources of vitamin B12 include:

⇨ yeast extract, such as Marmite

⇨ breakfast cereals fortified with vitamin B12

⇨ soya products fortified with vitamin B12.

Adults need about 1.5 micrograms of vitamin B12 a day. Check the labels of fortified foods to see how much vitamin B12 they contain.

What are good vegetarian sources of omega-3 fatty acids?

Sources of omega-3 fatty acids suitable for vegetarians and vegans include:

⇨ flaxseed oil

⇨ rapeseed oil

⇨ soya oil and soya-based foods (such as tofu)

⇨ walnuts.

Omega-3 enriched eggs are also a good source if you are a vegetarian and include eggs in your diet.

Evidence suggests that the type of omega-3 fatty acids found in these foods may not have the same benefits for reducing the risk of heart disease as those found in oily fish.

However, if you follow a vegetarian diet, you can look after your heart by eating at least five portions of a variety of fruit and vegetables every day, cutting down on food that is high in saturated fat and watching how much salt you eat.

What are good sources of protein for vegetarians?

Most vegetarians have enough protein in the diet. Good sources of protein for vegetarians include:

⇨ nuts and seeds

⇨ pulses and beans

⇨ soya products (tofu, soya drinks and textured soya protein, such as soya mince)

⇨ cereals (wheat, oats and rice)

⇨ eggs

⇨ reduced-fat dairy products (milk, cheese and yoghurt).

A variety of protein from different sources is necessary to get the right mixture of amino acids, which are used to build and repair the body's cells.

Are Quorn products suitable for vegans?

No. Since all Quorn products contain a small amount of egg white and most also contain milk ingredients, they are not suitable for vegans. However, they can be a source of protein for vegetarians.

Do I need a special diet if I exercise?

You don't need a special diet for exercising if you're a vegetarian or vegan. The advice for vegetarians who exercise is the same as the advice for non-vegetarians who exercise regularly.

Most vegetarians have enough protein in their diet for the body to grow and repair itself. If you exercise regularly, make sure you eat plenty of complex carbohydrates such as rice and pasta for energy, and drink enough fluids when exercising harder.

Is it healthier to eat organic fruit and vegetables?

Vitamin and mineral levels in food vary depending on the soil the plants were grown in, when they were picked and how they were stored. There's no scientific evidence that organic food is healthier. Eating organic is a personal choice and many people eat organic for environmental reasons. It's important to eat plenty of fruit and vegetables whether they're organic or not.

19 October 2013

⇨ The above information is reprinted with kind permission from NHS Choices. Please visit www.nhs.uk for further information.

The best countries in the world for vegetarians

Glasgow has been heralded as the best city in the world for vegans, but where are the best nations for travellers on a meat-free diet?

By Jane Hughes

So now that we've established – or at least PETA has – that Glasgow is the most vegetarian/vegan-friendly place in the UK the next question is, which the best country for vegetarians and vegans? In many countries, eating meat is part of the national identity. Think of Australian barbecues, American cowboys and South American cattle ranchers. There was controversy earlier this year when President Obama hosted a dinner for 12 Republican senators, and one of them ordered a vegetarian meal. The identity of the culprit was protected, for fear that exposure could mean losing their seat. TV host Bill Maher commented that American voters would sooner elect a gay president than a vegetarian. Republican senators in Iowa and Texas said vegetarians were 'un-American' and made public pledges to eat more meat.

Still, once you've waved the political madness aside, you'll find that cutting-edge vegetarian and vegan cuisine thrives on America's east and west coasts. San Francisco still benefits from its hippie heritage with decent vegetarian and vegan options as standard around the Haight. San Francisco's Zen Center established Greens in 1976, and various cookbooks from its resident chefs continue to influence the menus of vegetarian eateries worldwide. Millennium, in the city centre, ranks as one of the world's top vegan restaurants with impressive high-end cuisine. Seattle and Portland are hot spots, with vegan bakeries, breweries, clothing stores, bike shops and even – in Portland – a vegan strip joint. However, PETA's choice for the top city in the US this year was, surprisingly, Austin, Texas. In the heart of ranching country, vegan entrepreneurs have taken to the streets with food trucks offering tempeh burritos and chicken faux-jitas. It can still be a struggle to find vegetarian food in small-town diners, and it makes most sense to look for sustenance in areas that are highly populated and diverse: big cosmopolitan cities are the best place to look for vegetarian and vegan food.

Barcelona is fast becoming a hot spot for vegetarians, whether your preference is for punk bars or candle lit fine dining. Elsewhere in Spain, it can be a struggle to explain that vegetarians don't eat ham. Likewise Berlin, another city where countercultures thrive, offers a good deal more for the vegetarian or vegan visitor than more rural German towns. France is notoriously hard work for vegetarians, and it can be far easier to settle for an omelette than to brave the ire of a waiter in a high-end French restaurant, but Paris has more than 30 exclusively vegetarian eateries. Even Russia, where vegetarianism was actually banned and driven underground for decades after the revolution, offers enough meat-free dining experiences in St Petersburg and Moscow to keep vegetarian visitors out of a rut for a week or so.

Any bustling city with a diverse population, cultural leanings and a university or two can generally be relied upon to offer a few exclusively vegetarian cafes, but often the food on offer is disappointingly divorced from the national cuisine. Falafels and hummus, veggie burgers, pizza, pasta and Indian-style buffets are pretty standard all over the place, but getting a vegetarian meal in, for example, a restaurant that specialises in typical Danish food can be very hard work. Vegetarian visitors to Denmark tend to rely on curry houses and Turkish kebab shops that offer falafels, tabbouleh and salad-filled pittas. There's no history of meat-free eating in Belgium – even the chips are often cooked in lard. Belgian vegetarian food makes frequent use of seitan, a surprisingly realistic meat substitute made from wheat gluten. Against all odds, the EVA (Ethisch Vegetarisch Alternatief) has persuaded many cafes and restaurants in its home town, Ghent, to adopt Paul McCartney's Meat-Free Monday idea and serve vegetarian food one day a week – in this case, Thursdays. Ghent also has more vegetarian restaurants per capita than most cities (13 for a population of 240,000).

Of course, there are many parts of the world where vegetarianism is widespread, largely because of religious principles and dietary laws. Hindus, Jains and Taoists all advocate vegetarianism to a greater or lesser extent, and this has a positive effect on the availability of vegetarian food in India and Asia. Between 20% and 40% of India's population is vegetarian – the figure is muddied by the fact that most Indian Hindus do not consider people who eat eggs to be vegetarian. Clear food labelling laws make things easy for vegetarian visitors. Most of the food served at Sikh gurdwaras is vegetarian, not because Sikhs are required to be vegetarian but because they aim to offer food that is acceptable to as many people as possible.

Countries with large Buddhist populations are generally good destinations for vegetarians, although the Buddhist approach to vegetarianism varies and is often misunderstood. The Theravada tradition, dominant in Thailand, teaches that it is all right to eat meat if it is offered to you, the Mahayana Buddhists of Taiwan, Vietnam and Japan recommend vegetarianism, and Tibetan Vajravana Buddhists consider vegetarianism optional. Being vegetarian would have been tricky in a mountainous region centuries ago, so it's hardly surprising that countries with climates that support plentiful harvests of fruit and vegetables tend to have more of a history of vegetarianism than those whose inhabitants are forced to rely on eating fish or animals that do not require lush grazing land.

Vegetarian travellers can also benefit from religious dietary observations that don't directly advocate vegetarianism. In Israel, Kashrut laws require that meat and dairy produce are not served together, making it relatively easy to find vegetarian food. In some African countries, such as Ethiopia, the Christian faith calls for frequent days of fasting, when only meat-free or vegan meals are acceptable.

British vegetarianism has Christian roots, too. Abstinence from meat was considered a form of temperance in the early 1800s, and over the years many radical thinkers embraced the idea. During the Second World War, rationing conferred luxury status on meat, but interest in vegetarianism perked up again in the 1960s, thanks to trendsetters such as the Beatles, who brought the idea to a new audience. In today's multicultural society, it is easy to find meat-free specialities from all over the world. Add to that clear labelling regulations, and the UK has to be one of the easiest places in the world to be vegetarian.

23 September 2013

⇨ The above information is reprinted with kind permission from *The Guardian*. Please visit www.theguardian.com for further information.

Number of global vegetarian food and drink product launches doubles between 2009 and 2013

As World Vegetarian Day is recognised (1 October) around the globe, it seems that more products than ever are showcasing vegetarian credentials. Indeed, new research from Mintel has found that 12% of global food and drink products launched in 2013 carried a vegetarian claim, up from 6% in 2009. Further to this, 2% of global food and drink launches carried a vegan claim in 2013, up from 1% in 2009.

Today in Britain, the vegetarian diet is firmly on the map with 12% of UK adults following a vegetarian or vegan diet, rising to 20% of 16 to 24s. In the UK alone, Mintel estimates the meat-free food market to have hit £625 million in 2013 and further forecasts it to rise to £657 in 2014, up from £543 million in 2009. Indeed, Mintel's research reveals that almost half (48%) of Brits see meat-free products as environmentally friendly and 52% see them as healthy.

Laura Jones, Global Food Science Analyst at Mintel, said:

'As World Vegetarian Day arrives, our research highlights just how much of an impact vegetarianism has had on the UK food and drink market. Globally, the outlook for the meat alternative market is positive and will continue to be driven by an emerging consumer trend towards meat reduction on a part-time basis, also called flexitarianism, entailing increased consumption of plant-based foods without completely cutting out meat. Indeed, many meat-reducing consumers have adopted a flexible attitude, choosing to limit meat, rather than eliminate it entirely. Launches of vegetarian and vegan products echo manufacturers' desire to communicate the suitability of their products to the widest range of consumers.'

In addition, whilst it has been a concern for vegetarians that they will miss out on a vital source of protein, just 17% of Brits who are consuming less protein than they were a year ago say this is because they are following more of a vegetarian diet. Moreover, whilst the benefits of protein have been in the spotlight over the past 12 months, many Brits are opting for non-meat protein sources with one in eight (18%) Brits claiming they are eating more non-animal sources of protein (e.g. dairy, plant, grains) compared to a year ago. Despite this, in 2013 less than 1% of food and drink products launched globally carried both a 'vegetarian' and 'high-protein' claim.

'Plant-based and other vegetarian protein sources align with consumer interest in reducing red meat consumption and growing interest in vegetarian products. Indeed, consumers are shifting towards more plant-based diets.' Laura continues.

Signifying the rise of the 'flexitarian', there seems to be a trend for consumers to embrace more vegetable-based meat dishes. Today, as many as one in eight (13%) UK meat-buyers claim they would be interested in buying half and half products from the supermarket, with 50% red meat and 50% vegetable protein for example.

In addition to the rise of vegetarian protein sources, there has also been considerable growth in the number of chocolate and sugar confectionery products launched carrying a 'vegetarian' or 'vegan' claim. Whilst just 4% of chocolate or sugar products launched in 2009 carried a vegetarian claim, this rose to 9% in 2013. The proportion of these products launched with a vegan claim similarly rose from 1% in 2009 to 2% in 2013.

Further to this, the number of chocolate and sugar confectionery products using a glazing agent boasted even larger growth with 32% of these products carrying a 'vegetarian' or 'vegan' claim in 2013, up from 13% in 2009.

'Among chocolate and sugar confectionery products there is increasingly demand for vegetarian ingredients, reflected by the increasing use of both vegetarian and vegan claims on new product launches. Ingredients will continue to be scrutinised by consumers and manufacturers need to be responsive and proactive to quell any consumer concerns.' Laura concludes.

Mintel is the world's leading market intelligence agency. For over 40 years, Mintel's expert analysis of the highest quality data and market research has directly impacted on client success.

1 October 2014

⇨ The above information is reprinted with kind permission from Mintel. Please visit www.mintel.com for further information.

Should everyone become vegetarian?

With ethical diets on the increase among young voters, we talk to them about what they eat and why it matters politically.

In our 'Virgin voters' series, we listen to what young people and first-time voters have to say about the issues that matter most to them. With increasing numbers of students supporting the Green party and environmental causes, we ask young people about their attitude towards meat.

Vegetarian, vegan, flexitarian: what's going on?

⇨ Vegetarian diets are gaining in popularity, with 12% of UK adults following a vegetarian or vegan diet, according to research published last year. Millions more are flexitarians, cutting down on meat. Environmental or health concerns are given as reasons.

⇨ Young people in particular are adapting their diet according to environmental beliefs, with 20% of 16- to 24-year-olds following a vegetarian diet. The Vegetarian Society says: 'Young people have increased their awareness of the environmental impact of eating meat from 8% in 2007 to 40% in 2013.'

What the political parties are saying:

⇨ The Green party supports 'a progressive transition from diets dominated by meat and other animal products to healthier diets based on plant foods' and 'more sustainable methods of production such as organic and stock-free farming'. It would ensure vegetarian and vegan options are available in schools, hospitals and other public sector establishments.

⇨ The Conservatives and Labour have no clear policies on vegetarianism, though both support sustainable farming.

The Lib Dems also care about sustainability and say they want to improve welfare conditions for animals kept on farms. UKIP wants to ban religious slaughter for halal and kosher meat where animals are killed without being stunned – but a Lib Dem MEP says this is 'more about exploiting xenophobia than protecting animals'.

We spoke to young people to find out how important ethical food consumption is to them: what do they eat and do they think politicians should talk more about where our food comes from?

'Everyone should cut down on meat – western meat-eating levels are unsustainable'

Jess Murray, 19, philosophy student at University College London (UCL), is vegan. She says:

Becoming vegan was an ethical decision. I wanted to avoid killing animals just because I wanted – rather than needed – to eat them. I moved from being vegetarian to vegan as I realised that vegetarianism does little in terms of animal rights – people tend to up their dairy intake as vegetarians, and the dairy industry is filled with cruelty. It's hard to justify the meat and dairy industries as they currently stand, because the animals are treated badly, and unless you have the money, it's hard to obtain ethically sourced meat. Everyone should cut down on their meat consumption, as current western meat-eating levels are at an unsustainable level.

'It's selfish and unethical for humans to kill animals for food'

Jena Herbert, 21, a PGCE student at University College London (UCL), is vegetarian. She says:

I've been vegetarian all my life – almost 22 years. Just like us, animals have feelings and suffer considerably due to the meat industry, and it seems to me to be selfish and unethical for humans to continue to kill animals for food when there are so many wonderful alternatives out there now. I'd never say that everyone should eat in the same way as me. I do think, however, that it would be good for our planet if more people thought more carefully about, not only where their food comes from, but also how it ends up on your plate. I believe that many of my friends would cut down on their meat intake if they saw some of the inhumane methods undertaken in slaughterhouses.

'I'd like more emphasis to be put on the environment in politics'

Frederick Wilson-Hafffenden, 22, Cambridge graduate working for an educational startup, eats meat. He says:

I eat meat because I believe it to be healthy and I enjoy it, but I don't think you need it with every meal. I probably eat it once a day. Everyone should know where their meat is from – animal welfare is very important, as is humane slaughter. I don't buy organic meat but always buy free-range meat, and my family eat the meat from our farm.

Having grown up around animals and seen both organic and non-organic produce, I think non-organic gives the animals a more comfortable life. It allows 'chemical' medicines to be used in the same way that we use 'chemical' medicines on humans, rather than finding a naturally occurring compound to attempt to do the same job. Buying local produce is also important. I'd like more emphasis to be put on the environment in politics.

'The welfare of animals and the environment is low down on most people's list of priorities'

Meriel, 22, Exeter graduate and project assistant for the Imperial War Museum, is flexitarian. She says:

I've been a semi-vegetarian since I was ten. I eat fish and poultry, but don't eat meat from livestock such as lamb, pork or beef. I'm quite strict with it – if I order chicken in a restaurant, I check that the gravy doesn't use beef-stock, but I won't have a meltdown if I eat sweets with gelatine in. I often just say I'm vegetarian so I don't have to ask awkward questions about ingredients. What I eat is now out of habit, rather than principle, and it's the texture and smell of meat I can't stand.

People should be aware of where their food comes from, but I think that unfortunately politicians would be wasting their breath promoting it in their campaigns. It could make such a difference to our nation's health, the welfare of animals, and the welfare of the environment if we ate less meat and only produced as much as is sustainable. Sadly, these things are very low down on most people's priorities.

'I don't care too much about where my meat comes from'

Benjamin Macey, 19, first-year pharmacy student at the University of Bath, eats meat. He says:

I enjoy eating meat because of the taste and I believe it's essential for a balanced diet. I don't really have any ethical concerns and don't care too much about where my meat comes from. I wasn't bothered by the horse meat scandal either because horse meat can be healthier than beef.

However, I try to buy British and organic where possible to support our farmers. The only environment issues I'd be interested in hearing more about from politicians would be the problems of waste, landfill and the packaging the food comes in.

'Politicians' attitudes towards ethical food consumption and the environment considerably affect my vote'

Molly Russell, 18, first-year French and English literature student at the University of Warwick, is vegetarian. She says:

I've been vegetarian for ten years and am currently following a vegan diet a couple of days a week. For me, the reasons are purely ethical and environmental. At the age of eight I became interested in environmental issues, animal rights and the harsh reality of factory farming. Eating meat contributes to land and water pollution and the needless suffering of animals. If people considered more deeply where their food came from, they'd think about reducing their meat intake.

I strongly believe these issues should feature more on the political agenda. Politicians' attitudes towards ethical food consumption and the environment considerably affect my vote, and for this reason I am planning on supporting the Green party in this year's general election.

'Not everyone has the time or money to follow a vegetarian diet'

Helena Horton, 20, third-year philosophy student at the University of York, is vegetarian. She says:

I've been vegetarian since I was eight. Eating animals is gross and sad, and the meat industry is bad for the environment and harmful to animals. Paul McCartney said: 'If abattoirs had glass walls, then we would all be vegetarian.' People should cut down on meat, but I understand that not everyone can afford the time or money to follow a vegetarian diet.

The issue should possibly be higher on the political agenda, though there are arguably more important things happening, such as the rise in the need for food banks.

How important is ethical food consumption to you? Do you feel that these issues should be higher up on the political agenda?

10 August 2014

⇨ The above information is reprinted with kind permission from *The Guardian*. Please visit www.theguardian.com for further information.

Should 'real men' be vegetarians?

By Jon Young

Earlier this year I decided to become a vegetarian. It's not a typical choice for a 35-year-old male – particularly a former 'lad' like me. But after learning about the journey our meat makes on the way to the dinner table, it was the only sensible choice. I expected a level of debate, but I didn't expect some of the gender stereotypes that came my way. Apparently, meat-eating is an essential part of being a man. Eating a rare steak, burning sausages on the barbecue and having a fondness for pork scratchings are all part of the criteria. Meat keeps you strong. If you don't eat it you won't be able to hold a drill, to till the field, or keep the door open for those poor weak women.

It's been an eye-opener noticing how central eating meat is to male identity. I have begun to understand how frustrating it must be for women when their gender gets in the way of their achievements. But fighting through the haze of stereotypes and misinformation, of course, is the irrefutable logic that becoming a vegetarian is a good thing, regardless of your gender. The truth will always win eventually, and here are a few of its ingredients:

1. The natural order: One of the biggest pro meat-eating arguments is that it is natural to do so. Yet, our biology suggests otherwise. Our closest relative in the animal kingdom – the chimpanzee – is an omnivore with a diet of less than 10% meat. Our digestive system is far more similar to herbivores than carnivores. We do not have nails or teeth that can tear apart raw meat, and our stomachs do not have the hydrochloric acid that carnivores' do to break meat down. Carnivores' intestines are short, to dispose of meat quickly – ours are long to absorb nutrients through water (better suited to fruit and vegetables).

2. Nutrition: Another common argument is that we need meat to enjoy a balanced diet. But the main things meat provides us with – protein, iron and vitamin B12 – are abundant in beans, leafy greens and eggs.

    There is significant evidence that vegetarianism is healthier. Saturated fat found in meat is the biggest driver of high cholesterol and therefore high blood pressure, strokes and heart disease. There have been many examples of people making a full recovery from heart problems when moving to a meat-free diet, compared to limited success when they don't.

3. Animal cruelty: Of course, for many, the main reason for becoming vegetarian is the animal cruelty in meat production. Chickens, cows, pigs and sheep typically live in horrendous, unnatural conditions to line corporation pockets and to give us cheap meat at dinner time. A recent investigation by Animal Aid showed that although required by law, stunning does not always take place at UK slaughterhouses. There are many other examples that show the same. And spare a thought for the centrepiece of our Christmas dinner (the turkey) which in representing a feast of love, has been fattened to the extent that it can no longer fly, breed or in some cases, stand.

4. The environment: Finally, of course, there is the damage to the environment. Meat production is the second biggest contributor to environmental problems on all levels. It has a devastating impact on land degradation, water pollution and biodiversity of species. Livestock pollution alone is responsible for 18% of greenhouse gas emissions. A study in the States showed that if every American swapped one meal of chicken a week for non-meat it would be the same as taking half a million cars off the road.

The above only scratches the surface. I would recommend John Robbins' *The Food Revolution* or Allen Carr's *Lose Weight Now* if you want a more complete picture.

So where does this leave the masculinity debate? Well as long as people think that chewing on a chicken's leg is an essential part of manhood, social pressure will probably come out on top. But perhaps we can create an alternative gender justification? The same people who say real men eat meat also think that men should look after and protect people who are close to them. So let's ensure we protect our loved ones by eating a healthier diet. Let's also protect them by helping to create an environment with reduced global warming. Real men, they say, should not use their physical strength to gain an advantage over others. So let's extend this protection to defenceless animals.

Of course, I don't really believe eating meat (or not) has anything to do with masculinity. Gender rules are as limiting for society as national and racial stereotypes. The long-term goal is surely to remove attachment to masculinity altogether.

6 July 2015

⇨ The above information is reprinted with kind permission from the author, Jon Young. You can follow Jon Young on Twitter: www.twitter.com/JEGyoung or at http://www.huffingtonpost.co.uk/jon-young/.

Should we all become vegans to save the planet?

A study into the greenhouse gas emissions caused by different types of diet has for the first time provided quantitative evidence that going meat-free can dramatically reduce environmental impact. The paper, published in the journal *Climatic Change*, analysed data from the diets of 65,000 meat eaters, fish eaters, vegetarians and vegans, and found the greenhouse gas emissions for a meat-based diet were approximately twice as high as those for vegans, and about 50 per cent higher than for vegetarians.

One of the authors of the paper, Dr Peter Scarborough, spoke to the Oxford Martin School's Communications Officer, Sally Stewart, about the research and its implications.

What led you to undertake this study?

Our research at the British Heart Foundation Centre on Population Approaches for Non-Communicable Disease Prevention has shown that, in addition to reducing the likelihood of developing cardiovascular disease, changes to diet and nutrition can bring about improvements in a wide range of areas. Because what we eat has such a large carbon footprint associated with it, one of the areas that changing your diet can have an impact on is environmental sustainability. It's an issue which is only going to become more and more important, and there's a lot of research taking place at the moment into what a sustainable, healthy diet actually looks like.

So what's different about this paper?

We've known for quite some time about the greenhouse gas intensity of the production of different foods. But what we haven't had a good grasp on is the difference in the greenhouse gas emissions caused by different diets. In the absence of this data, what researchers have generally done is to construct a vegetarian diet or vegan diet, for instance changing meat with vegetables or cheese, which doesn't realistically construct what a real vegetarian diet would look like.

By collaborating with researchers here in Oxford who are working on cancer epidemiology we have been able to get access to very good data from the EPIC-Oxford Study, which looks at how diet influences the risk of developing cancer. So we didn't have to construct any diets, these people were actually meat-eaters, or vegetarians or vegans, giving you genuine diet comparisons. The diet data is actually from a while ago and average meat consumption has gone up since then, so if anything the results are actually an underestimation of the impact. And from a previous study, which looked at the effect of applying a greenhouse gas tax to foods, we had the knowledge of the emissions caused by different types of foods.

What impact do you want this research to have?

As I mentioned before there is a push at the moment on trying to design what a healthy sustainable diet is, and making sure that knowledge is included in government advice on eating. This already happens in The Netherlands where the advice is to eat less meat, and in Italy there is government guidance on the sustainability of different food groups. In the UK the Food Climate Research Network is doing a lot of very good work in terms of trying to build a consensus on what a healthy, sustainable diet looks like.

How much impact have government recommendations such as those in The Netherlands and Italy actually had on people's behaviour?

In terms of sustainability we are not yet sure, but what making this kind of advice part of government guidance does is provide a solid bedrock to create interventions. Until something is enshrined in a recommendation we are still going to be moving around the question of what a sustainable healthy diet is. Once that's concreted into official advice saying you can reduce your environmental impact and improve your health then you can look at interventions.

What sort of form might these take – are we talking about telling people what they can and can't eat?

We're just at the stage of brainstorming about this. You can intervene on lots of different levels – national trade agreements, food labelling, taxation. No-one's talking about those at the moment because it's not mainstream enough. What's important right now is to build the support. Interventions could also be at an individual level, for example with mobile phone apps or building an online social community.

You could also look at the institutional level, such as bringing in 'meat-free Mondays', or for catering companies to look at providing mainly vegetarian food and having to opt in to have meat. But actually the message from the paper is just to reduce your meat consumption. We're not telling people they have to give up meat completely; just cutting down makes a big difference.

Reference

Scarborough P, Appleby P, Mizdrak A, Briggs A, Travis R, Bradbury K, Key T. *Dietary greenhouse gas emissions of UK meat-eaters, fish-eaters, vegetarians and vegans. Climatic Change*, 2014; 125(2):179-192.

17 July 2014

⇨ The above information is reprinted with kind permission from the Oxford Martin School. Please visit www.oxfordmartin.ox.ac.uk/opinion/view/262 for further information.

Meat in your diet

Meat is a good source of protein, vitamins and minerals in your diet. However, the Department of Health has advised that people who eat a lot of red and processed meat a day (more than 90g cooked weight) cut down to 70g.

Making healthier choices can help you eat meat as part of a healthy, balanced diet. But some meats are high in saturated fat, which can raise blood cholesterol levels.

If you eat a lot of red and processed meat, it is recommended that you cut down as there is likely to be a link between red and processed meat and bowel cancer.

Meats such as chicken, pork, lamb and beef are all rich in protein. A balanced diet can include protein from meat, as well as from non-animal sources such as beans and pulses.

Red meat provides us with iron, and meat is also one of the main sources of vitamin B12.

Food hygiene is important when storing, preparing and cooking meat.

Meat and saturated fat

Some meats are high in fat, especially saturated fat. Eating a lot of saturated fat can raise cholesterol levels in the blood, and having high cholesterol raises your risk of heart disease.

The type of meat product you choose and how you cook it can make a big difference to the saturated fat content.

Make healthier choices when buying meat

When buying meat, go for the leanest option. As a rule, the more white you can see on meat, the more fat it contains. For example, back bacon contains less fat than streaky bacon.

These tips can help you buy healthier options:

⇨ Ask your butcher for a lean cut.

⇨ If you're buying pre-packed meat, check the nutrition label to see how much fat it contains and compare products.

⇨ Go for turkey and chicken without the skin as these are lower in fat (or remove the skin before cooking).

⇨ Try to limit processed meat products such as sausages, salami, pâté and beefburgers, because these are generally high in fat. They are often high in salt, too.

⇨ Try to limit meat products in pastry, such as pies and sausage rolls, because they are often high in fat and salt.

Cut down on fat when cooking meat

Cut off any visible fat and skin before cooking – crackling and poultry skin are much higher in fat than the meat itself.

Here are some other ways to reduce fat when cooking meat:

⇨ Grill meat, rather than frying. Trimmed pork chops that have been grilled contain around one-third the fat of roasted untrimmed chops. A lean grilled rump steak contains about half the fat of fried

rump steak with the fat. And fried chicken breast in breadcrumbs contains nearly six times as much fat as chicken breast grilled without the skin.

⇨ Don't add extra fat or oil when cooking meat.

⇨ Roast meat on a metal rack above a roasting tin so the fat can run off.

⇨ Try using smaller quantities of meat and more vegetables, pulses and starchy foods in dishes such as stews, curries and casseroles.

How much red and processed meat should we eat?

Red meat (such as beef, lamb and pork) can form part of a healthy diet. But eating a lot of red and processed meat probably increases your risk of bowel (colorectal) cancer.

Processed meat refers to meat that has been preserved by smoking, curing, salting or adding preservatives. This includes sausages, bacon, ham, salami and pâtés.

If you currently eat more than 90g (cooked weight) of red and processed meat a day, the Department of Health advises that you cut down to 70g.

90g is equivalent to around three thinly cut slices of beef, lamb or pork, where each slice is about the size of half a piece of sliced bread. A cooked breakfast containing two typical British sausages and two rashers of bacon is equivalent to 130g.

Storing meat safely

It's important to store and prepare meat safely to stop bacteria from spreading and to avoid food poisoning:

⇨ Store raw meat or raw poultry in clean sealed containers on the bottom shelf of the fridge, so the meat can't touch or drip onto other food.

- Follow any storage instructions on the label and don't eat meat after its 'use by' date.

- If you cook meat that you're not going to eat straight away, cool it as quickly as possible and then put it in the fridge or freezer. Remember to keep cooked meat separate from raw meat.

- Always thoroughly clean plates, utensils, surfaces and hands straight away after they have touched raw or thawing meat to stop bacteria from spreading.

Freezing meat safely

It's safe to freeze raw meat providing that you:

- Freeze it before the 'use by' date.

- Follow any freezing or thawing instructions on the label.

- Cook the meat straight away if you defrost it in a microwave. If you want to defrost meat and cook it later, thaw it in a fridge so that it doesn't get too warm.

- Use the meat within two days of defrosting. It will go off in the same way as fresh meat.

- Cook food until it's steaming hot all the way through.

- When meat thaws, liquid can come out of it. This liquid will spread bacteria to any food, plates or surfaces that it touches. Keep the meat in a sealed container at the bottom of the fridge so that it can't touch or drip onto other foods.

- If you defrost raw meat and then cook it thoroughly, you can freeze it again. But never reheat meat or any other food more than once as this could lead to food poisoning.

Cooking meat safely

Some people wash meat before they cook it, but this actually increases your risk of food poisoning, because the water droplets splash onto surfaces and can contaminate them with bacteria. For this reason, it's best not to wash meat.

It's important to prepare and cook meat properly. Cooking meat properly ensures that harmful bacteria on the meat are killed. If meat isn't cooked all the way through, these bacteria may cause food poisoning.

Bacteria and viruses can be found all the way through certain meat. This means you need to cook these sorts of meat all the way through. When meat is cooked all the way through, its juices run clear and there is no pink or red meat left inside.

Meats that you should cook all the way through are:

- poultry and game, such as chicken, turkey, duck and goose, including liver

- pork

- offal, including liver

- burgers and sausages

- kebabs

- rolled joints of meat.

You can eat whole cuts of beef or lamb when they are pink inside – or 'rare' – as long as they are cooked on the outside. This is because any bacteria are generally on the outside of the meat.

These meats include:

- steaks

- cutlets

- joints.

Liver and liver products

Liver and liver products, such as liver pâté and liver sausage, are a good source of iron, as well as being a rich source of vitamin A.

You should be able to get all the vitamin A you need from your daily diet. Adults need:

- 700 micrograms of vitamin A per day for men

- 600 micrograms of vitamin A per day for women.

However, because they are such a rich source of vitamin A, we should be careful not to eat too much liver and liver product foods because over the years, a harmful level of vitamin A can build up in the body. This is because the body stores any vitamin A it doesn't use for future use, which means you do not need to consume it every day.

Having too much vitamin A – more than 1.5mg of vitamin A per day from food and supplements – over many years may make your bones more likely to fracture when you are older.

People who eat liver or liver pâté once a week may be having more than an average of 1.5mg of vitamin A per day. If you eat liver or liver products every week, you may want to consider cutting back or not eating them as often. Also, avoid taking any supplements that contain vitamin A and fish liver oils, which are also high in vitamin A.

Women who have been through the menopause and older men should avoid having more than 1.5mg of vitamin A per week from food and supplements. This means not eating liver and liver products more than once a week, or having smaller portions. It also means not taking any supplements containing vitamin A, including fish liver oil, if they do eat liver once a week. This is because older people are at a higher risk of bone fracture.

Pregnant women should avoid vitamin A supplements and liver products.

Eating meat when you're pregnant

Meat can generally be part of a pregnant woman's diet. However, pregnant women should avoid:

- Raw and undercooked meat, due to the risk of toxoplasmosis. Make sure any meat you eat is well cooked before eating.

- Pâté of all types, including vegetable pâté. They can contain listeria, a type of bacteria that could harm your unborn baby.

- Liver and liver products. These foods are very high in vitamin A, and too much vitamin A can harm the unborn child.

3 July 2015

- The above information is reprinted with kind permission from NHS Choices. Please visit www.nhs.uk for further information.

UN report concludes Europeans should cut meat and dairy consumption by half

A new report commissioned by the United Nations Economic Commission for Europe has found that if Europeans reduced their consumption of meat and dairy by half, it would cut nitrogen pollution and greenhouse gas emissions from agriculture by around 40 per cent, as well as benefit our health.

Nitrogen on the Table: The influence of food choices on nitrogen emissions and the European environment, which is to be published next month, notes that animal farming is a major source of ammonia, nitrates and other nitrogen-based compounds that pollute our air and water. Therefore, halving our consumption of animal products and switching to more plant-based agriculture would significantly cut nitrogen pollution rates. As animal farming is also a major source of greenhouse gas emissions (14.5 per cent globally) it goes on to say that halving meat and dairy consumption would be a significant step towards meeting climate change targets.

The report also points out that reducing meat and dairy consumption by half would bring European diets much closer in line with dietary recommendations from bodies such as the World Health Organization and World Cancer Research Fund, based on intakes of saturated fat and red meat. This means it would not only be good for the environment, but benefit public health too.

A shift towards a more plant-based diet would also free up huge areas of agricultural land currently being used to grow feed for animals. This land, the report states, could be used to grow more cereal crops for export, as well as bioenergy crops, thus reducing our dependence on fossil fuels. The EU could also cut imports of soya beans by around 75 per cent, the cultivation of which is a leading cause of deforestation around the world.

28 April 2014

⇨ The above information is reprinted with kind permission from Animal Aid. Please visit www.animalaid.org.uk for further information.

Meat is a complex health issue but a simple climate one: the world needs to eat less of it

THE CONVERSATION

An article from The Conversation.

By Dora Marinova, Professor of Sustainability at Curtin University and Talia Raphaely, Lecturer, Curtin University

Climate change is the greatest challenge to human health, according to the recent Lancet Commission report which calls for action to protect the global population. The report says that tackling climate change could deliver huge public health benefits, largely through phasing out coal, embracing renewable energy, and moving to a low-carbon economy. There is, however, one crucial issue the report fails to address: meat.

The Commission's recommendations are all based on solid evidence about the link between greenhouse gas emissions, global warming and human health. Focusing only on energy policy, however, will not be enough to head off climate change successfully. Calls for action that do not include reduction in the world's livestock production and meat consumption will not be able to protect public health from the effects of climate change.

The livestock sector is a large source of global greenhouse gas emissions, with estimates of its overall contribution varying between 18% and 51%. Even in the smallest estimate, the livestock sector emits more greenhouse gas than the world's transport networks.

According to one set of projections, by 2050 this sector will single-handedly account for 72% of the total 'safe operating space' for human-caused greenhouse gas emissions, 88% of the safe operating space for biomass use, and 300% of the safe operating space for the mobilisation of nitrogen compounds in soils and elsewhere. This would lead to irreversible changes, irrespective of any efforts to mitigate climate change in other sectors of the economy.

The livestock industry does not just generate carbon dioxide – it adds to the full spectrum of major greenhouse gases. It is the primary (and growing) source of methane and nitrous oxide – gases estimated to have 84 and 264 times respectively the global warming potential of CO_2 on a 20-year horizon.

On the positive side, however, methane dissipates the most rapidly of all greenhouse gases, and so changing what we eat would have an also immediate effect on climate change. Moving away from meat would also help farmers to use nitrogen more efficiently, which would have the dual impact of causing less pollution while also helping people get more nutrition from the foods they grow.

Not just about animal welfare

Since the 1970s, meat has been seen as problematic from an animal welfare perspective. In recent decades, however, it has transformed into environmental concerns, as we realise the huge and unprecedented future impacts of meat consumption on the climate.

The meat issue also now includes questions about international food security, which will become more of a challenge given the impending damage to ecosystem services and the fact that meat is an inefficient way to produce calories anyway. Concerns about dependency, distribution and corruption in food supply are justified, but in a world facing rapid global climate change with increasingly stressed ecosystems and a growing human population, the rationale for eating less meat is clear.

This is just as true in export markets, such as Australia's sales to China, as it is for domestic consumption. Livestock, like mining, is an industry in which Australia is 'offshoring' large amounts of greenhouse emissions.

Meat and health: a tricky question

Perhaps the reason the Lancet Commission chose to stay away from the meat issue is because there is not a straightforward, universal relationship between meat and health. Levels of animal protein intake vary significantly across the globe. In poor countries such as Chad or Bangladesh, eating meat might be a question of survival.

Animals slaughtered worldwide
Official and estimated data, 2011

1,383,000,000 Pigs

24,000,000 Buffalo

296,000,000 Cattle

654,000,000 Turkeys

517,000,000 Sheep

430,000,000 Goats

649,000,000 Geese & Guinea Fowl

2,817,000,000 Ducks

58,110,000,000 Chickens

Source: Meat Atlas, facts and figures about the animals we eat, *Friends of the Earth Europe,* January 2014

Meanwhile, people in the developed world, including Australians, are consuming meat far beyond healthy levels. Australia's dietary guidelines suggest limiting red meat intake to 455g per week (65g per day) to reduce cancer and cardiovascular risk, but Australians eat 42% more than this, and yet more meat is produced but wasted.

While the Food and Agriculture Organization rightly says that people should 'have access to a diverse range of nutritious foods and to the knowledge and information... to make healthy choices', many people still choose cheap, meat-based options that increase the burden on both ecosystems and health systems.

Few people consciously consider the planetary impact of the meat products they eat. The evidence however is clear: Earth cannot continue to support a population of seven billion people and the 70 billion animals they raise and slaughter each year for food.

At the moment the problem is getting worse, not better: meat consumption is growing faster than the overall population.

Whether or not one cares about one's own personal health and well-being, achieving long-term population health and stabilising climate change require serious reduction in global meat consumption. As ever, the biggest potential for change is among those who can most afford it and are most responsible for the current problem. Cutting down on meat is where the best public health opportunity lies in relation to climate change.

5 July 2015

The hidden costs of steak

The price tag on a package of meat does not reflect the true cost of producing the contents: the hidden costs to the environment and the taxpayer are much higher. If these costs are included, livestock raising would probably make a net loss. Around 1.3 billion people worldwide live from animal husbandry – most of them in developing countries. The majority graze their animals on land around the village, some move from place to place with their herds, and others keep a few chickens, cattle or pigs near their homes. In the developed world and rapidly growing economies, the number of livestock keepers is falling. The livestock sector is becoming industrialized and meat producing companies are expanding.

The profits of these companies are not just a result of their own efforts. They are also built on the environmental damage caused by factory farming and the use of livestock feed – costs that the companies do not have to pay. In addition, they receive subsidies from the state. These subsidies are often distributed true to the motto: the bigger the company, the higher the subsidy. No consolidated economic and ecological accounting has yet been done, but we can discern its broad outlines. When an animal product is purchased, three prices have to be paid: one by the consumer, one by the taxpayer and one by nature. The consumer uses the first price to judge the item's value. The other two prices represent hidden subsidies to the people who produce and merchandise it.

The costs borne by the environment are probably the biggest, but they are hard to calculate. Over the last three decades, economists and accountants have developed their own 'environmental-economic accounting' that estimates damage to nature in monetary terms. It covers the costs of factory farming that do not appear on the company's balance sheet, such as money saved by keeping the animals in appalling conditions. Costs to nature are incurred by over-fertilisation caused by spreading manure and slurry on the land and applying fertilisers to grow fodder maize and other crops. If the quality of water in a well declines because of high nitrate content, the costs are hard to calculate: they often are only recognised when the well has to be capped and drinking water shipped in from somewhere else. Other externalities – costs that do not appear in the consumer price – arise if over-fertilisation means the soil can no longer function as a filter for rainwater, if erosion carries it away, if biodiversity declines, or if algal blooms kill fish and deter tourists.

However, for the majority, the most extensive damage occurs further away from the cause. Intensive livestock production releases nitrogen compounds such as ammonia into the atmosphere, contributing markedly to climate change. According to the European Nitrogen Assessment in 2011, this damage amounted to some 70 to 320 billion dollars in Europe. The authors of this study concluded that this sum could exceed all the profits made in the continent's agricultural sector. If this were counted, the sector as a whole would make a loss.

In China, the immediate costs of over-fertilisation are estimated at 4.5 billion dollars a year, mainly because water quality suffers from intensive livestock production. The main problem is that in rapidly developing areas of East Asia, farmers and agricultural firms are replacing the traditional organic fertilisers – manure and faeces – with synthetic nitrogen. Manure, which used to be considered the best type

of fertiliser in integrated farming, now has to be disposed of somehow – in a river, on a dump, or trucked to where it can be used. To ensure the highest yields, the fields are fertilized with commercial agrochemicals containing readily soluble nutrients as well. This results in a double burden on the environment. Cheap meat is made possible only by polluting the environment.

The other big unknown in the real price of meat are subsidies using public funds. A package of subsidies may consist of many different components. The European Union offers subsidies for fodder crops and supports up to 40 per cent of the cost of investing in new animal housing. A crisis fund, set up in 2013, can be used to support factory farms, for example to support the export of meat and milk powder.

Further burdens are heaped onto national taxpayers. They pay for the costs of transport infrastructure, such as ports needed to handle the feed trade. In many countries, meat is subject to a reduced level of value added tax. In addition, low wages in abattoirs make it possible to produce meat cheaply. From a political point of view, low wages can be seen as subsidies because companies can pay so little only if the state does not impose a statutory minimum wage. Few poor countries can subsidise their farmers in this way. Instead, they tend to support them through laws that permit the exploitation of people and the environment. To remain the cheapest suppliers of feed or meat in the world market, governments allow workers to toil in slave-like conditions and for little pay, they lease government land to large-scale producers at cheap rates, and they fail to act against loggers who clear areas of land for ranchers to occupy.

January 2014

⇨ The above information is reprinted with kind permission from Friends of the Earth Europe. Please visit www.foeeurope.org for further information.

Lessons to learn about meat and the world

1 **Diet is not just a private matter.**
Each meal has very real effects on the lives of people around the world, on the environment, biodiversity and the climate that are not taken into account when tucking into a piece of meat.

2 Water, forests, land use, climate and biodiversity:
The evironment could easily be protected
by eating less meat, produced in a different way.

3 The middle classes around the world eat too much meat.
Not only in America and Europe, but increasingly in China, India and other emerging countries as well.

4 **High meat consumption leads to industrialised agriculture.**
A few international corporations benefit and further expand their market power.

5 Consumption is rising mainly because **city dwellers are eating more meat.** Population growth plays a major role.

6 Compared to other agricultural sectors, poultry production has the strongest international links, is most dominated by large producers and has the highest growth rates. **Small-scale producers, the poultry and the environment suffer.**

7 **Intensively produced meat is not healthy** – through the use of antibiotics and hormones, as well as the overuse of agrochemicals in feed production.

8 Urban and small-scale rural livestock can make an important **contribution to poverty reduction, gender equality and a healthy diet** – not only in developing countries.

9 Eating meat does not have to damage the climate and the environment.
A few international corporations benefit and further expand their market power.

10 Alternatives to meat exist. Many existing initiatives and certification **schemes show what a different type of meat production might look like** – one that respects environmental and health considerations provides appropriate conditions for animals.

11 **Change is possible.** Some say that meat consumption patterns cannot be changed. But a whole movement of people are now eating less meat, or no meat at all. To them it is not a sacrifice; it is part of **healthy living and a modern lifestyle.**

Source: Meat Atlas, facts and figures about the animals we eat, *Friends of the Earth Europe*, January 2014

Flexitarianism: the environmentally friendly diet

Most people are by now familiar with the concept of vegetarians, people who don't eat meat or fish. They will also recognise vegans, people who don't eat any animal products, and maybe pescitarians, people who don't eat meat, but do eat fish.

There is a new dietary choice that has been gaining awareness and acceptance alongside these: flexitarianism. Known by a few other names (flexible vegetarian, demitarian, semi-vegetarian, part-time carnivore, etc.), a flexitarian has a mainly plant-based diet, but eats small amounts of, probably higher standard, meat, fish and dairy.

On the rise

The flexitarian diet is becoming an increasingly popular choice. The global trend is showing an increase in meat eating, but in certain parts of the world, like the UK, meat consumption has declined. The average amount of meat and dairy consumed each week in the UK has dropped from 1,160g per person in 1980, to 989g in 2012. This declining trend is due to a number of reasons: health benefits of lower meat diets, the higher cost of meat and dairy, food scares such as the horsemeat scandal and the environment impact of livestock production. It looks like this trend might continue: a recent YouGov survey conducted for Eating Better found that 25 per cent of the British Public had cut back on meat in the past year, and that 34 per cent would consider eating less meat in the future.

Flexitarianism is being predicated as the next big foodie trend. You can find the newly accepted word in the *Oxford English Dictionary* (and also on sites like Urban Dictionary), excellent blogs (like http://theflexitarian.co.uk) and hundreds of flexitarian cook books to choose from. Celebrity chefs such as Yotam Ottolenghi regularly include meat-free and low meat dishes on his menus and in his columns, and Michel Roux Junior has been talking about the need to reduce our meat consumption on programmes like *BBC Food & Drink*.

Restaurants such as The Grain Store and River Cottage are promoting sustainable diets, with a wide range of meat-free and low meat dishes on the menu.

What's the gain?

A flexitarian diet for all, as well as benefiting our health, is necessary to enable us to feed the growing global population within planetary boundaries. There will be an estimated extra two billion people globally by 2050, meaning the food system will need to feed over nine billion people. The UN Food and Agricultural Organisation (FAO) estimates that this will require overall food production to increase by about 70% by 2050, with an extra 200 million tonnes of meat produced to meet the growing demand. Yet this assumes significant increases in meat consumption whilst more affluent countries maintain current levels.

By switching to flexitarian diets in high meat-eating regions like the UK we can ease the pressure on the global food systems, and feed more people without destroying the environment.

So what does being a flexitarian mean? Practically?

It's a personal choice, but having a flexitarian diet could mean:

⇨ Meat and dairy free before 6pm

⇨ Meat free during the week: only eating meat at the weekends

⇨ Using meat as a flavour, not the base of the meal

⇨ Only eating meat dishes three times a week.

It is really up to you and your tastes and preferences, but they all have one thing in common. They involve cutting down how much meat, dairy and fish we eat.

Why go flexitarian?

1. Livestock and climate change

Our agricultural systems are one of the biggest emitters of greenhouse gasses, with livestock production accounting for 14.5 per cent – 21 per cent of global greenhouse gas (GHG) emissions according to the FAO. These emissions come for a wide range of sources, the largest of which (45 per cent of the total emissions) is attributed to growing the feed for livestock. Producing just 1 kilogram of soyabeans (a common component of animal feed) releases 7.7 kilograms of GHG. Other sources include deforestation for farming land (9 per cent), emissions from the animals themselves (39 per cent) and manure decomposition (10 per cent).

Switching to a lower meat diet, reducing intake from over 100g per day to less than 50g per day can cut GHG by nearly half. A reduction in our meat and dairy consumption has been identified by the IPCC as a significant step we can all take to reduce our GHG emissions, and will be a necessary if we want global temperatures to stay below 2°C of warming.

2. Livestock and land use

Land is a finite resource, with a large number of demands competing for space, like food production, housing, biofuels and nature. Our ability to feed the global population comes into direct conflict with these demands, especially our ecosystems and the demand for biofuels. Land for livestock and the production of animal feed is a key driver of deforestation. In Brazil alone, 62.2 per cent of deforested land is used for pasture for cattle, and the Chaco region in South America, 63 hectares of forest is cleared every hour, meaning an area over ten times the size of Hyde Park in London is destroyed each day.

The amount of land used in livestock production is already huge, eating up 75 per cent of all current agricultural land usexi, a third of which is used to grow animal feed. By reducing the global consumption of animal products by just ten per cent, we could free up enough land to enable us to feed an extra four billion people just using the agricultural land already in use.

Land used for growing animal feed and for livestock rearing could be converted to the cultivation of crops for human consumption instead.

A flexitarian diet would also reduce the pressure on our scarce freshwater supplies. Over extraction and climate change have severely depleted the global reserves of fresh water, so much so that a third of the world does not have enough water. Agriculture consumes 70 per cent of the global freshwater supply, a third of this is on livestock production. It takes 15,455 litres of water to produce one kilogram of beef, compared to 255 litres for a kilogram of potatoes.

3. Livestock and health

Meat is a good source of protein, iron and other nutrients that are essential to a balance, and healthy diet. However, there is an established link between overconsumption of meat and a long list of health problems, like an increased risk of heart disease, strokes and obesity. Excessive consumption of meat has also been linked to an increased risk of cancer. Research by Friends of the Earth suggests that a low meat diet could prevent over 45,000 premature deaths, and save the NHS over £1.2 billion per year.

It is not just about the amount that we eat either. Processed meats are much higher in salt, sugar and fat, as well as having less protein per kilogram. Excessive consumption of red meat has also been linked to an increased risk of cancer. The Department of Health guidelines state that people should only eat 70g of red and processed meat

a day, a figure back by the World Cancer Research Fund. Eating less, and better, meat is better for our health.

Alongside the effects that overconsumption of meat can have on individual health, the widespread use of antibiotics in farming is contributing to a growing threat to global health. Large volumes of antibiotics are used in farming, but not just for treating sick animals. They are administered as a preventative measure to stop the rapid spread of disease in intensely farmed livestock. The unregulated overuse of antibiotics in farming around the globe is exacerbating the problem of antibiotic-resistant bacteria, and is a key source of antibiotic resistance in common bacteria, such as salmonella. This is hurting our ability to fight diseases we thought we had treatments for, and the World Health Organization warns that we are heading for a 'post-antibiotic era – in which common infections and minor injuries can kill'.

4. Fish

The technology supporting fishing has become more and more sophisticated, with fleets using sonar to pinpoint the exact location of fish shoals they use methods such as pair trawling, with nets that can fit ten Boeing jumbo jets or bottom trawling, that drag along the floor and completely destroy sea bed habitats to catch huge numbers of fish. This has led to the collapse of fish stocks, with the FAO classing over 70 per cent of the world's fish stocks as 'fully exploited', 'over exploited' or 'depleted'. This is not only a tragedy for our marine ecosystems, but also for the many people around the world who rely on small-scale fishing for food and employment.

So why not cut it out entirely and go vegetarian?

Not all meat and dairy consumption and production is environmentally damaging. Intensive livestock production, with its huge environmental footprint and dependence on oil-based fertilisers, chemicals and imported feeds, is not compatible with a low-carbon future.

However, not all farming methods are the same: farming in smaller quantities, letting livestock graze instead of housing them intensively in sheds and feeding them imported crops can all reduce the environmental impact of meat and dairy production.

Livestock farming has an important role in many people's lives around the world. It provides livelihoods for around one billion of the world's poorest people, as well as being a vital part of many people's diets.

Part of a sustainable diet

While flexitarianism can have a significant positive impact on our health and the planet, it should form part of a wider sustainable diet. Alongside eating less meat, it includes:

⇨ Eating more plant based foods

⇨ Eating better meat

⇨ Wasting less food

⇨ Eating more fresh food and less processed food

⇨ Sourcing from known suppliers that have good standards.

Adopting a sustainable diet is one way for individuals to tackle catastrophic climate change and the environmental damage caused by our current diets. Friends of the Earth is also calling for action at a local, national and global level to support sustainable diets, from advocating change to international agricultural standards, to getting the UK Government to commit to promoting sustainable diets through guidelines and procurement standards.

July 2014

⇨ The above information is reprinted with kind permission from Friends of the Earth England, Wales & Northern Ireland. Please visit www.foe.co.uk for further information.

Top food trends for 2015

By Natural Balance Foods and Lucy-Ann Prideaux

Last year, quinoa and kale were the hot topic, so what does 2015 have in in store for us? Expert Nutritionist, Lucy-Ann gives us her predictions...

It appears that many of us suffer from a condition called 'restless palate syndrome' – a term coined by food analysts to describe our ever-increasing desire to try new or exotic foods, unusual or particularly nutrient-dense foods, or our need to find new ways of impressing our friends. Chefs are heavily in the act, spurring many of us on to try novel ingredients, as restaurateurs try and tempt new customers through the door and stay ahead of rivals and competitors.

All this underpins, and drives new food trends across the board, from food retail and food service, to food manufacture. Here's a taster of what to expect and look out for in 2015.

Hybrid vegetables

Not content with nature's creations, we seem to be in the throes of an increased production of 'hybrid vegetables'. Crossing one vegetable with another to enhance the nutritional value, versatility or appeal of vegetables, is set to top the list of food trends in 2015. New veggies you will see appearing include kalettes (a cross between kale and Brussels sprouts), rainbow carrots, broccolini (broccoli crossed with Chinese broccoli), and broccoflower (broccoli crossed with cauliflower). Like it or not, tinkering with Mother Nature is an area of food production that is expanding.

'Ugly' vegetables

We may see more 'ugly' vegetables in the shops too, as these are also set to become trendier in 2015, amongst chefs and consumers alike. Ugly vegetables include the knobbly celeriac, kohlrabi, as well as the humble parsnip. Chefs again will show us the way in terms of how to cook these fantastic plant foods. Of course these vegetables are not new to devoted plant-based eaters, and I for one, love 'ugly veg'! There's a myriad of ways to eat them too. Celeriac and parsnips make the most delicious 'oven chips', simply chopped into chunky strips, sprinkled with sea salt and black pepper and dry-roasted in the oven. They can also be mashed, pureed, fried or baked and even flavoured with honey and spices! So next time you pass the 'ugly veg' in the shopping aisle, take your pick and give them a go!

Fermented foods

You may have already noticed that Japanese cuisine (including fermented foods and sushi) is on the up, with more Japanese restaurants popping up, along with Japanese foods on the shop shelves. We appear to love all things Japanese!

If you're unsure as to what exactly fermented produce is, this area covers a number of foods and products from yogurts to certain breads (e.g. sourdough bread), as well as pickled vegetables, vinegars and the Japanese products tofu, miso, tempeh and tamari. All these are examples of foods that are fermented naturally with bacterial cultures. Fermentation is an old way of preserving food and shelf life, and populations the world over have used fermentation methods for centuries. One of the key attractions nowadays, driving the trend in fermented foods, is how they benefit intestinal health.

Eating fermented foods such as 'live' yogurt for example helps to boost levels of beneficial bacteria and/or optimise the pH of the gut. Our gut 'beneficial bacteria' aid digestion, boost immunity and even lead to increased production of certain vitamins. Many fermented

foods are, however, heavily salted (think of sauerkraut and tamari), so whilst they are beneficial in small amounts and used as 'condiments', eating them in moderation is the key.

Healthy snacks

Other trends set to increase include gluten-free foods, 'healthy snacks' such as our very own Nakd and Trek bars, frozen foods for 'locked-in freshness', protein-rich foods, protein-boosted flours and, of course, dairy-free milks. There will also be more of a focus on plant-based proteins, and guess what... pistachios are tipped to be 'the nut of 2015'!

Dips, desserts and artisan breads

Something which may float your boat is the upcoming trend of vegetable ice-creams, and even vegetable yogurts. How does tomato or carrot ice-cream sound?! Maybe you'd prefer a tomato yogurt, butternut squash yogurt, beet, carrot or kimchee yogurt? Good news or bad, these new products are set to hit the UK shelves pretty soon!

We will also be seeing lots of different kinds of hummus, artichoke and guacamole-style dips, flavoured again with different herbs and spices. One new spice to hit the shelves is the Middle Eastern blend, za'atar.

Lastly, 'artisan breads' will expand, along with new-fangled toast toppings and sandwich fillings! Personally, I am quite happy with a little rye bread topped with avocado, tomato and watercress. I am not entirely sure I'll be tempted by a filling of 'smoked kale jelly'!

⇨ The above information is reprinted with kind permission from Natural Balance Foods. Please visit www.naturalbalancefoods.co.uk for further information.

© Natural Balance Foods 2015

Top five worst celebrity diets to avoid in 2015

The British Dietetic Association (BDA) is today revealing its annual list of *Top Celebrity Diets to Avoid in the New Year*. This year, making a brand new entry, the Urine Therapy Diet has taken the top slot, followed by the Paleo Diet at number two, the Sugar Free Diet at number three, the VB6 Diet at number four and completing the list this year is the Clay Cleanse Diet.

The British Dietetic Association, founded in 1936, is the professional association for dietitians in Great Britain and Northern Ireland. It is the nation's largest organisation of food and nutrition professionals with over 7,500 members. The BDA is also an active trade union.

That time of the year is just around the corner: the New Year. The Christmas festivities have been and gone, the partying is a distant blur, everyone seems to have a case of the post-Christmas blues and this year, yes this year, you will get the body of your dreams! 2015 is your time! But how?

Yes, the New Year and January means a media frenzy of 'New Year, New You', which undoubtedly involves the latest magical ways to losing weight. However, with so many diet books and celebrity-endorsed fitness DVDs on the market, how do you ensure you lose lbs, instead of £s.

The BDA receives literally hundreds of calls from the media every year on this subject and they come across a huge range of weird and whacky diets and diet claims.

Based on telephone calls and other contributing factors, here are the top five dodgy celeb diets to avoid in 2015:

Urine Therapy

Celebrity link: Bear Grylls has reportedly drunk his own urine (for his TV show).

What's it all about? Urine Therapy, or urotherapy, includes the drinking of one's own urine for cosmetic or medical/wellbeing purposes. Some claim that the urea component of urine can have an anti-cancer effect.

BDA verdict: Literally, don't take the proverbial! Emergencies only, as Urine Therapy has no scientific evidence that it adds anything beneficial to the body and its safety has not been established. As for any anti-cancer claims made in favour of Urine Therapy, this is simply not backed up by scientific studies.

Paleo Diet

Celebrity link: Miley Cyrus and Matthew McConaughey have reportedly followed this 'diet'.

What's it all about? The Paleo Diet (also known as the Paleolithic Diet, the Caveman Diet and the Stone Age Diet) is a diet where only foods presumed to be available to Neanderthals in the prehistoric era are consumed and all other foods, such as dairy products, grains, sugar, legumes, 'processed' oils, salt and others like alcohol or coffee are excluded.

BDA verdict: Jurassic fad! A diet with fewer processed foods, less sugar and salt is actually a good idea, but unless for medical reason, there is absolutely no need to cut any food group out of your diet. In fact, by cutting out dairy completely from the diet, without very careful substitution, you could be in danger of compromising your bone health because of a lack of calcium. An unbalanced, time consuming, socially isolating diet, which this could easily be, is a sure-fire way to develop nutrient deficiencies, which can compromise health and your relationship with food.

Sugar Free Diet

Celebrity link: Tom Hanks and Alec Baldwin have reportedly followed this 'diet'.

What's it all about? The Sugar Free Diet is when you exclude all types of sugar (and often all carbohydrates too) from your diet.

BDA verdict: Not a total sweetener for success! We encourage cutting down on free sugars, adding sugar or products already containing added sugar, in addition to being label aware, because as a nation, we consume too much sugar on the whole. Some versions of the Sugar Free Diet call for you to cut out all sugar from your diet which is not only almost impossible, but would mean cutting out foods like vegetables, fruit, dairy products, nuts – not exactly a healthy, balanced diet. Also beware, substitutes some of these plans recommend like agave, palm sugar or honey, are actually just sugar in another form and a huge contradiction.

Vb6 Diet

Celebrity link: Beyoncé and Dita Von Teese have reportedly followed this 'diet'.

What's it all about? The VB6 Diet (vegan before 6pm) of Chegan Diet (cheating vegan) is a diet that calls on you to follow a vegan eating plan most of the time/before 6pm, then after 6pm, nothing is off limits.

BDA verdict: VB careful! By virtue, this should set you on course to eating during the day, at least, less processed food, more plant-based foods like beans, pulses, wholegrains and nuts (watch your portion sizes) and much more fruit and vegetables which is a good thing overall as we should be aiming for at least five portions of fruit and veg a day and more fibre. Having said that, following a vegan diet doesn't automatically translate into a healthy diet. The danger here is, post-6pm becomes a window of opportunity to hoover up a myriad of foods high in calories, saturated fat and packed with added salt and sugar, undoing your earlier healthier choices. The reality is, eating different food groups at different times of the day doesn't matter, in terms of your health, it's nutritional balance that's important.

The Clay Cleanse Diet

Celebrity link: Zoe Kravitz has reportedly followed this 'diet'.

What's it all about? A spoon of clay a day will remove toxins from the body and remove negative isotopes, helping you detox and stay in shape

BDA verdict: Clay away from this diet! The Food Standards Agency issued a warning about clay after high levels of lead and arsenic were discovered in products saying: 'We remind consumers, especially pregnant women, about the dangers of ingesting clay, clay-based detox drinks and supplements'. The whole idea of detox is nonsense. The body is a well-developed system that has its own built-in mechanisms to detoxify and remove waste and toxins. Nuff said!

BDA spokesperson and consultant dietitian, Sian Porter added:

'Every year in the BDA press office, we get call after call about all sorts of diets, from the weird and faddy right through to the downright dangerous, such as the Breatharian Diet that calls on people to live on fresh air and sunlight alone! 2014 has been no exception.

'It seems that as a nation we are constantly on the search for that magic bullet approach to losing weight, wanting a quick fix to give us the bodies we so often see on TV, in glossy magazines and adorning billboards up and down the UK.

'Quite often the fad diets we come across come at a price. Firstly, there can often be a cost to your health if you follow these diets over a period of time and secondly, there are often accompanying books, products, paid-for memberships or online services that can quickly add up. The truth is, if something sounds too good to be true, it probably is.

'When wanting to lose some weight, don't think about 'going on a diet' or just what changes you need to make over a month or two to lose the weight, think about what changes you need to make forever to lose that weight and, as importantly, keep it off. An eating pattern for life should be the one you can stick to and include enjoyment, a rich variety of foods in appropriate portion sizes and moderation. Go for the marathon approach rather than the sprint finish.

'2015 is almost upon us, with many people making New Year resolutions to lose. Make the difference this time by losing it in a safe, robust and sustainable way.

8 December 2014

⇨ The above information is reprinted with kind permission from BDA The Association of UK Dietitians. Please visit www.bda.uk.com for further information.

Should you go on a wheat-free diet?

By Natural Balance Foods and Lucy-Ann Prideaux

A wheat-free diet has many health benefits, but it's important to know the facts. Here our nutritionist Lucy-Ann Prideaux reveals all you need to know about wheat, and healthy snacking.

Wheat and gluten are often used interchangeably, but it's important to understand that whilst wheat and gluten do go 'hand in hand', these are two distinct different groups of proteins. Gluten is not just present in wheat; it's also present in other grains too, such as barley, rye, oats, spelt and kamut grain. Wheat (and therefore gluten), is present in thousands of everyday foods worldwide including breads and bread products, cakes, biscuits and bars, buns, pizzas, wraps, rolls and a great majority of processed foods. As some of you may be aware, even simple packaged foods such as soups, ready meals and sweets contain fillers such as wheat flour, and therefore contain gluten too!

Why do so many choose to eat a diet free from wheat and gluten?

Here are some documented problems associated with eating wheat:

⇨ Wheat is a common food allergen, causing digestive, immune-related and weight problems in many.

⇨ According to Dr William Davis, author of *Wheat Belly*, gluten also appears to be an appetite stimulant...

⇨ Wheat is addictive too! Gluten-derived polypeptides can cross into the brain and bind to the brain's opiate receptors. The result is a mild euphoria after eating a product made with wheat.

⇨ Wheat also contains a starch called amylopectin A, which is quickly converted to blood sugar. This leads to a fast, and high rise in blood sugar and insulin; commonly linked to the development of diabetes, weight gain and obesity.

⇨ Wheat contains a particular lectin (a protein) called WGA. WGA is largely responsible for many of wheat's ill effects such as gut inflammation, and digestive complaints.

⇨ Recent research has shown that wheat consumption in 'healthy normals' causes a condition called leaky gut.

⇨ Leaky gut tends to promote low-grade inflammation, which is an underlying characteristic of heart disease, cancer and autoimmune problems.

⇨ High wheat-based diets often have a high glycaemic index, or 'High GI'. High GI diets are linked to obesity and diabetes.

⇨ Wheat contains a substance called phytate, which may lead to reduced absorption of minerals such as zinc and iron.

What about gluten specifically?

Gluten can pose a serious threat for those with a diagnosed gluten allergy, commonly known as coeliac disease. The protein acts like a poison to the lining of the gut, creating inflammation, damage and decay to the cells. As you might expect, this causes serious digestive and health complications. However, what is becoming more common, and more apparent to doctors and other health professionals is the increasing incidence of gluten 'intolerance' or sensitivity, whereby gluten is being identified as a significant contributor to health and gut problems (e.g. leaky gut), even without a positive test for full-blown gluten allergy.

Why has gluten become such a problematic dietary substance?

Here are some likely reasons:

⇨ Our lack of genetic adaptation to grasses and grains, particularly wheat.

⇨ The hybridisation of wheat, and the resulting higher gluten content of many common, everyday foods.

⇨ The sheer volume of grains and grain-based foods in modern-day diets.

Are wheat and gluten causing you unnecessary problems?

The only way one can really tell, if gluten, wheat, or any food or substance, is a significant cause of your health or gut problems, is to eliminate it from the diet. Whilst testing can certainly help identify gluten sensitivity, the only way a person will really know if gluten is problematic is by doing the gold standard 'allergy test' – i.e. eliminating the suspect food for two to four weeks. Gluten is the not the easiest thing to take out of the diet, although, given a little direction, it is relatively simple, and certainly do-able. The results for many people are well worth the effort. Remember that gluten is not just present in wheat. It is part of other grains too, such as barley, spelt, rye and even oats, as well as many products. Whilst some gluten-intolerant individuals can tolerate some oats in the diet, I suggest trying one week totally gluten-free. Be very aware of the 'hidden' sources of gluten, found in soups, tinned foods, and soup mixes, and even non-food related products such as lipsticks!

The benefits of a wheat and gluten-free diet

⇨ Improved digestion and digestive function – a crucial aspect of effective weight loss is a healthy and efficient digestive system.

⇨ Excess fluid loss and weight loss.

⇨ Increased energy.

⇨ Better bowel function and elimination.

⇨ Improved mental function and better mood!

⇨ The above information is reprinted with kind permission from Natural Balance Foods. Please visit www.naturalbalancefoods.co.uk for further information.

© Natural Balance Foods 2015

The great gluten-free scam

Once, pasta and bread were store cupboard staples. Now, many of us are replacing them with 'healthier' gluten-free foods. But are they really better for us?

By Julia Llewellyn Smith

Staples such as bread (-8.9 per cent) and pasta (-4.2 per cent) suffered a decline in sales over 2014, while the 'free-from' food category – including dairy-free and gluten-free products – went from niche to mainstream.

'Free-from' sales topped £0.5 billion for the first time after sales grew by 15 per cent, reports market research company Neilsen, which analysed purchasing trends in Britain's ten largest supermarkets, excluding discounters Aldi and Lidl.

Less than two per cent of the population has a food allergy, but millions more believe they suffer from the condition and they are proving to be a lucrative market for manufacturers.

In a corner of my local, shabby Tesco, whole new ranges of biscuits, breads, cereal bars and even fish fingers have suddenly arrived, all stocked under the label 'gluten-free'.

Starbucks around the corner is suddenly offering gluten-free sandwiches, Carluccio's has gluten-free pasta. A local church, I hear, has sourced gluten-free communion wafers made from potato. In the United States, friends tell me, there are even gluten-free dating sites, uniting enemies of all that's dough-based.

Gluten-free food, not so long ago a niche product for hippies and those with coeliac disease, is the sustenance of the moment. Socialite Nicole Richie rapped about 'chillin' in my crib makin' gluten-free spaghetti'. Gwyneth Paltrow has put her children on a no-gluten diet.

Novak Djokovic, who attributes his gluten-free regime to transforming his tennis, now has his dog following it (though Andy Murray who beat him in this year's Wimbledon final says the same diet made him 'lose strength'.)

Even *The Great British Bake Off* recently devoted its quarter final to 'free-from' cakes and loaves.

Perhaps my muscle aches and worsening hay fever aren't the result – as I feared – of incipient middle age, but of my fondness for bread's springy texture, something gluten makes possible. If only I could renounce it, maybe my health would improve.

I'm not alone in my doubts: every week another friend (usually one who's been vegan and who's done every diet from Atkins to the 5:2) serves me quinoa or macaroons – two gluten-free staples. In a recent survey, more than 25 per cent of Americans claimed they were trying to cut down on gluten or avoid it completely.

It's increasingly easy to do so. While once gluten-free products were available only in the dusty corners of health-food shops, today 80 per cent of all such products are sold in supermarkets. According to the Food Standards Agency, the British gluten-free market is worth £238 million annually and grew by more than 15 per cent last year.

In the US, it's worth around $2.6 billion, a growth of 36 per cent since 2006, with predictions it may double in size in the next two years. Across Europe, demand is soaring – with even carb-loving citizens of countries like Italy now demanding gluten-free pasta and pizza. India with its growing middle class is also touted as a potential huge market.

The new ubiquity of gluten-free products certainly makes life much easier for sufferers of coeliac disease, an auto-immune response to wheat where the body believes wrongly that gluten is attacking it. This makes the finger-shaped vilii that line the small intestine flatten out, stopping absorption of nutrients, with side effects including muscular disturbances, joint pain, headaches and vertigo.

But coeliacs make up only one in 100 of the population, while one in five of us is buying gluten-free products. Surveys of US consumers show that, of these, only five per cent are buying to combat coeliac disease, with the vast majority citing their reasons as 'digestive health', 'nutritional value' and 'to help me lose weight'. People have been eating bread since biblical times without reporting adverse effects. So why has it recently become demonised?

The gluten-free 'community' points to a recent surge in the number of people being diagnosed as coeliacs. Not so long ago GPs expected to see one case during their whole career, but now one per cent of the population has it. (Though others say the rise is simply due to improved diagnostic methods and greater awareness of the condition.)

'More and more people are coming to us saying they simply can't stomach industrial loaves,' says Chris Young, coordinator for the Real Bread campaign. The cause of the change, believes Young, is connected to the Chorleywood process, a technique launched by British bakers in 1961.

By juggling a cocktail of enzymes and artificial additives and introducing three times more yeast than had been used before, scientists at the Chorleywood Food Research Institute created a loaf that could be baked instantly without the need for the long 'prove' or ferment before going in the oven. The result was a loaf that lasted twice as long and was 40 per cent softer than previous types of bread.

'Bread is like fruit, it needs time to ripen and unfermented wheat appears to have a very bad effect on some digestive systems and in some cases triggers the coeliac response,' Young explains.

New, genetically modified 'dwarf' wheat, developed in the past 40 years may also have played a part. 'We used to grow wheat that was over 6ft tall, that was higher in nutrients and also contained a much smaller variety of gluten proteins than the dwarf varieties,' he says.

There's no conclusive research into these theories. 'We've challenged the big players, the food manufacturers for whom the bread industry's worth $3.2 billion annually to put money into this, to find out why so many people can no longer eat their products,' says Young. 'They just grumble there's no evidence fermentation brings benefits. But the reason there's no evidence is there's not enough research.'

What Young certainly isn't saying is that we should avoid all bread. He stresses that traditionally proven loaves – especially sourdough with its naturally occurring yeasts – appear to suit our digestive systems much better. 'People tell us all the time I can't eat factory bread, but when I go to France or Italy and shop at the little bakers, I have no problem.'

Nutritionist Ian Marber agrees that yeast, not gluten, may be the real culprit. 'Some people find that when they switch to a yeast-free bread, made from wheat or other grains, their bloating decreases, suggesting that the yeast and sugars used were the issue, not the grain. But, in practice, they stop eating bread, bloating stops, so the conclusion that wheat must be to blame is understandable, but misguided.' A coeliac himself, Marber is firmly of the opinion that while gluten intolerance – usually symptomised by bloating and abdominal pains – does exist, in general, wheat, and gluten in particular, have become a convenient scapegoat.

'We're always looking for something to blame for everything that's wrong in our lives and having a food intolerance is the holy grail. We can say: "It isn't the fact that I lie flat on my back and eat cream cakes all day that made me fat, it's the grilled aubergines I had for dinner last night. If I hadn't eaten them I'd be size eight and 6ft 3in."'

Gluten, he continues, is an easy target 'because it's so prevalent'. Many foods that contain gluten, like pizza, cakes and biscuits, are high in calories, so by avoiding them, many lose weight. 'If you make any adjustment to your diet, say you stop eating foods with the letter "l" in them, you may well lose weight, simply because you're making far better food choices than you were previously,' Marber says.

Marber acknowledges that gluten intolerance does exist, but probably in fewer cases than is generally believed. The only proper diagnosis for wheat intolerance is a test called a food challenge, carried out in a hospital. The patient is blindfolded and tested for wheat under controlled conditions, then monitored over three days to see if they develop any symptoms. Depending on which foods they react to, a food elimination programme is carried out under strict supervision.

Unsurprisingly, many prefer 'high-street' testing of the sort available in many health food stores. But this market is completely unregulated with most tests, according to a recent Which? report, producing usually 'highly inconsistent' results with no diagnostic value. Even more of us prefer self-diagnosis via 'Dr Google', as Marber calls it.

'They eat a huge bowl of pasta and experience lethargy, bloating, weight gain and decide they must have a food intolerance, but they've just eaten too much pasta.' In blind tests, three-quarters of people who believe they have an allergy or medical intolerance to bread show no signs of any symptoms.

While many of us are convinced that – coeliac or not – avoiding gluten will make us healthier, a study published last year in the *Journal of the Academy of Nutrition and Dietetics* disagrees. It concluded: 'There is no evidence to suggest following a gluten-free diet has any significant benefits in the general population.'

'Indeed,' it continued, 'there is some evidence to suggest that a gluten-free diet may adversely affect gut health in those without coeliac disease or gluten sensitivity.' Other research has indicated that gluten-free diets are often low in fibre and can be linked to deficiencies in B vitamins, iron and folate.

As Marber points out: 'If gluten really is the root of all evil, then coeliacs, who really can't eat it, would be in perfect health. I've been avoiding gluten since about 1823,' he jokes, 'but I still have all the normal aches and pains and health issues.' Yet the views of people like Marber won't prevent a tsunami of gluten-free products invading our supermarket. Several kitchen-table entrepreneurs who started making gluten-free loaves for coeliac relatives are now millionaires. Tesco peddles a heart-warming story of how its former chief executive Sir Terry Leahy appointed the mother of a child who suffered from several food allergies to set up his 'free-from' range, after she wrote to him complaining about the lack of suitable foods available.

But though he may have been moved by her plight, he almost certainly would have been excited by the commercial potential. A gluten-free label equates to a large mark up (though manufacturers argue that this is a result of higher production costs). Gluten-free Genius bread costs £3 a loaf in Tesco, compared with £1 for an ordinary loaf. Tesco's 'Free From' fusilli is £1.40, while a normal pack costs 95p.

Recently, US food giant General Mills boasted of double digit increases in sales of its Chex cereals after it was repositioned as gluten-free. Even products like humus, which have never contained gluten, are now being labelled 'gluten-free' by canny shopkeepers, to make them more attractive to the health conscious.

But a gluten-free label is no guarantee of virtuousness. While most dietitians would recommend someone with a genuine gluten intolerance focuses on a diet of fresh meats, fish, vegetables and unprocessed foods, the food industry prefers to market substitutes for 'banned' foods like biscuits, sausages, beer and ice cream – which many then believe, wrongly, they can eat guilt-free.

Dunkin' Donuts recently announced it's about to launch gluten-free doughnuts after years of failed attempts. Obstacles included the fact that gluten-free products are hard to mould into a circular doughnut shape and go stale quickly (because gluten holds in water).

Gluten-free products are frequently more adulterated and significantly higher in fat than their 'normal' equivalents. Gluten helps breads and bakery products retain their shape and softness as they cook, so to make up for its absence, manufacturers often use additives like xanthan gum and hydroxypropyl methyl cellulose or corn starch. Extra sugar and fat are often also added to make products tastier.

For example, Warburton's 'Free From' sliced white bread has 2.2g of fat per slice and 80 calories, compared with 1g per slice and 58 calories in its regular loaf. Young's gluten-free fish fingers contain 9.3g of fat per 100g, as opposed to 8.5g for the standard range.

Inevitably, in the US, a gluten-free backlash is already under way. 'Coeliac: the Trendy Disease for Rich, White People', is a typical recent headline in the popular blog, Science 2.0.

Unfortunately, the gluten-free community has even less tolerance for jokes than for pasta. American Idol host Ryan Seacrest was recently savaged on Twitter for his tweet about trendy new TV show Orange Is The New Black: 'Orange is the new black is the new gluten free diet', while the Disney Channel was forced to pull an episode of its children's show Jessie that made fun of a child with a long list of dietary requests, after outraged complaints from parents of gluten-intolerant children.

Marber predicts that these voices will only grow louder. 'Our attention will turn to other diet trends, but the gluten-free craze will grow and grow.' Following a gluten-free diet isn't actively harmful, he adds. 'If it makes you happy, do it!' he laughs. 'By buying that expensive stuff, you'll certainly be making someone else very happy.'

30 December 2014

⇨ The above information is reprinted with kind permission from *The Telegraph*. Please visit www.telegraph.co.uk for further information.

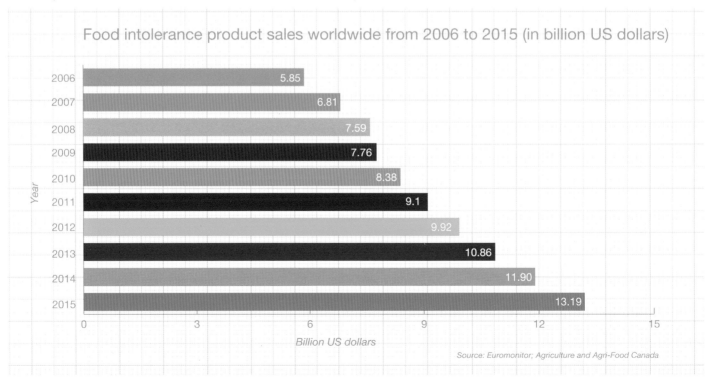

Food intolerance product sales worldwide from 2006 to 2015 (in billion US dollars)

Year	Billion US dollars
2006	5.85
2007	6.81
2008	7.59
2009	7.76
2010	8.38
2011	9.1
2012	9.92
2013	10.86
2014	11.90
2015	13.19

Source: Euromonitor; Agriculture and Agri-Food Canada

Orthorexia nervosa: when righteous eating becomes an obsession

***An article from* The Conversation.**

THE CONVERSATION

By Rebecca Charlotte Reynolds, nutrition lecturer at UNSW, Australia

Orthorexia nervosa, the 'health food eating disorder', gets its name from the Greek word *ortho*, meaning straight, proper or correct. This exaggerated focus on food can be seen today in some people who follow lifestyle movements such as 'raw', 'clean' and 'paleo'.

American doctor Steven Bratman coined the term 'orthorexia nervosa' in 1997 some time after his experience in a commune in upstate New York. It was there he developed an unhealthy obsession with eating 'proper' food:

'All I could think about was food. But even when I became aware that my scrabbling in the dirt after raw vegetables and wild plants had become an obsession, I found it terribly difficult to free myself. I had been seduced by righteous eating.'

Bratman's description draws parallels with many modern dietary fads that promise superior health by restricting whole food groups without a medical reason or even a valid scientific explanation.

Raw food followers might meet regularly to 'align their bodies, minds and souls' by feasting on 'cleansing and immune-boosting' raw foods. Such foods are never heated above 44°C, so 'all the living enzymes in the food remain intact'. No gluten, dairy or 'sugar' is allowed.

Clean eaters may follow similar regimes, removing gluten, dairy and even meat from their diets. You might overhear a discussion about 'superfood green smoothie' recipes after a yoga class that also happened to 'cleanse your gall bladder'.

And finally, around the corner, paleo pushers may 'beef up' together with a CrossFit class, followed by a few steaks. Again, with paleo, there is no gluten – or any grains for that matter – and no dairy or other such 'toxins' are allowed.

How common is orthorexia?

There is a blurry line separating 'normal' healthy eating and orthorexia nervosa, but one way to define the condition is when eating 'healthily' causes significant distress or negative consequences in a person's life.

They may be 'plunged into gloom' by eating a piece of bread, become anxious about when their next kale, chia or quinoa hit is coming, or eat only at home where 'superfood' intake can be tightly controlled.

Such behaviours can have a significant impact on relationships with family members and friends, let alone on their mental health.

Orthorexia nervosa is not a clinically recognised eating disorder but researchers have developed and tested questionnaires in various populations to get an idea of its prevalence.

Italian researchers developed the ORTO-15 questionnaire in 2005, with a cut-off score below 40 to signify orthorexia nervosa. Scores above 40 can still signify a tendency to pathological eating behaviours and/or obsessive-phobic personality traits.

Questions include: 'Does the thought about food worry you for more than three hours a day?' and 'Do you feel guilty when transgressing your healthy eating rules?'

Using this questionnaire and cut-off value of 40, another Italian research group reported a prevalence of orthorexia nervosa

of 57.6%, with a female-male ratio of two-to-one. However, using a cut-off value of 35, the prevalence reduced to 21%.

Most studies have been conducted in population sub-groups that may be at increased risk for orthorexia nervosa, such as health professionals. Again using the ORTO-15 and a cut-off value of 40, the prevalence of orthorexia nervosa in Turkish medical doctors was 45.5%, in Turkish performance artists it was 56.4% (81.8% in opera singers to 32.1% in ballet dancers) and in Ashtanga yoga teachers in Spain, 86.0%.

Using another questionnaire, the Bratman Test, 12.8% of Austrian dietitians were classified as having orthorexia.

You can test your own tendencies towards orthorexia nervosa using the Bratman Test and access support services via the National Eating Disorder Collaboration webpage and BodyMatters Australasia.

Is it a mental disorder?

Orthorexia nervosa is not listed in the American Psychiatric Association's *Diagnostic and Statistical Manual* (DSM-5), which psychologists and psychiatrists use to diagnose mental disorders. The DSM-5 currently lists anorexia nervosa, bulimia nervosa, binge-eating disorder, 'other specified feeding or eating disorder' and 'unspecified feeding or eating disorder'.

Some clinicians argue orthorexia nervosa should be recognised as a separate eating disorder and have proposed clinical DSM diagnostic criteria. They note distinct pathological behaviours with orthorexia nervosa, including a motivation for feelings of perfection or purity rather than weight loss, as they see with anorexia and bulimia.

Others disagree and argue that it falls in current eating disorder or other mental disorder categories. As Bratman explained in 2010:

'At times (but not at all times) orthorexia seems to have elements of OCD (obsessive compulsive disorder). It may also have elements of standard anorexia. But it is often not very much like typical OCD or typical anorexia.'

It's clear that more research is needed on orthorexia nervosa, including its diagnosis and potential DSM listing as an independent eating disorder.

It's also important to consider that people can move between mental disorder classifications. Sometimes labels may not be as important as providing solutions to patients with disordered eating, such as cognitive-behavioural therapy.

Striking a balance

As a nutritionist and a recovered sufferer of bulimia, I leave you with some advice:

Don't trust all devoted kale consumers, including health professionals and celebrities, if their advice isn't based on scientific evidence.

Don't make food the most important focus of your life. As Bratman says:

'Rather than eat my sprouts (or kale) alone, it would be better for me to share a pizza with some friends.'

Try to be a balanced food consumer with a 'mostly and sometimes' mantra.

26 March 2015

⇨ The above information is reprinted with kind permission from *The Conversation*. Please visit www.theconversation.com for further information.

Paleo Diet? Our bodies have moved on since the Stone Age

By Tim Spector

'Our ancestors didn't eat like this, so we shouldn't.' This is the main ethos of many modern diets which advise us to exclude a number of recent additions to our plates because they were not part of our distant predecessors' diet. There are many different variations on the theme – from all-encompassing 'palaeolithic-style' diets to grain-free or gluten-free regimes – which are all generating a massive boom in specialised shops, products and even restaurants.

The general idea is that for most of our millions of years of evolution we were not exposed to grains, milk, yogurt or cheese, refined carbs, legumes, coffee or alcohol. As they only came into existence with farming around 10,000 years ago, our finely-tuned bodies have not been designed to deal with them efficiently.

The belief is that human evolution via survival of the fittest and natural selection is a very slow process and our genes classically take tens of thousands of years to change. This means that these 'modern' foods cause various degrees of intolerance or allergic reactions, resulting not only in the modern epidemic of allergies, but also that the toxins lead

to inflammation and obesity. So follow our Palaeolithic ancestors we are told, cut out these foods – and your problems are over.

This may sound imminently sensible but as it turns out, the facts on which this idea is based are rubbish.

We have adapted

The latest research shows we are not robotic automatons fixed in time but flexible plastic beings adapting to our environments and diets much faster than anyone had realised. A study published in *Nature* showed clearly that major changes to our genes can occur in just 1,000 years or a few hundred generations.

The researchers looked at the DNA from 101 Bronze Age skeletons across Europe from The Netherlands to Russia for key mutations. These people lived around 3,000 years ago and were busy migrating and spreading their genes. They looked in particular at one key gene (called lactase persistence) that controlled an enzyme conferring the ability to digest milk after the age of three. Around three quarters of modern Europeans have this gene, allowing them to digest a glass of milk without feeling sick. Rates of the gene mutation are higher in North-Europe (up to 90%) and lower in Southern Europe (around 50%).

It was previously thought this gene mutation started to dominate Europeans around 7,000 to 10,000 years ago at the onset of farming and the use of milk, so the finding that only one in 20 Bronze Age people had it 3,000 years ago was a major shock. It meant that it started later and has spread much faster than we imagined and as a consequence we have adapted to our new food source much more rapidly than the lumbering robots we are portrayed as.

Other genetic evidence of recent changes to our digestive genes comes from a worldwide study of the amylase gene which is key to breaking down starch in carbohydrates. People in areas with starch as a major part of the diet evolved to have multiple copies of the gene to help them digest it better. We found in a collaborative study using our twins that this mutation also strangely protected against obesity, and importantly we think this change only happened in the last few hundred generations.

Other genes key to how we digest food can change even more rapidly. These are the 2 million or so genes in the DNA of the trillions of microbes in our gut. Although they are not human genes they are crucial to our health as they control our microbiome which digests our food and produces many of our vitamins and blood metabolites. These bacterial genes in our guts can respond rapidly to changes in our diet, and as they can produce a new generation every 30 minutes, they can evolve very fast indeed.

They also have a secret weapon called horizontal gene transfer which means they can rapidly swap genes between them to mutual advantage, without waiting for natural selection. They use this very effectively to become resistant to new antibiotics and the same process is likely for new foods.

So by all means enjoy eating at and going to trendy paleo steak restaurants and decide to lose weight in the short term by going on a gluten-free diet, but don't be fooled by the evolutionary scientific explanations which are now out of date. Your genes and your microbes are evolving faster than you realise and can cope with the new additions to our diet in the last few thousand years. The caveat is that we need to keep our gut microbes as healthy as possible. But dietary diversity, not exclusions, is the key.

24 June 2015

⇨ The above information is reprinted with kind permission from *The Independent*. Please visit www.independent.co.uk for further information.

Snacking on insects? Don't get bugged out

By Alisha Bhagat

Chewy and moist, the first bite didn't seem strange at all. Like any other energy bar it was dark and densely packed, with a slightly sticky texture. It was only a close examination of the wrapper that revealed that the special ingredient was ground cricket flour.

Last week, the US office engaged in an insect protein taste test. Inspired by the 2013 UN report about eating insects, as well as the spate of articles about eating insects in publications ranging from *Slate* to *The New York Times*, we wanted to see what all the fuss was about. The results were a little, well, disappointing.

We chose Chapul brand cricket bars primarily because they made eating insects seem easy. Unlike many insect foods that entail a whole bug (such as the sautéed grasshoppers at Brooklyn's Black Ant), cricket bars seemed easy on the squeamish eater. There were no exoskeletons to crunch or legs to chew on. The bars were like any other, and the flavours that came through were those of the other ingredients – peanut butter and chocolate for the Chaco bar. Eating insects was so easy – and tasteless – that it made me wonder why we were eating them at all. Vegetarian versions of the bars would have had all of the other ingredients: dates, peanuts, cocoa powder, honey, etc.

Insect eating proponents claim that getting bugs and beetles into our diets will alleviate the demand for conventionally-farmed meat and replace it with something that is good for the environment, low cost and healthy. While that is true, the challenge is to get people to actually eat them. Additionally, for all of the positive benefits to exist, people should be replacing conventional animal protein with insects, not eating them in lieu of plants.

And there's the rub, because for many westerners the thought of eating insects brings up a gag reflex. While the UN report states that there are two billion people around the world who eat insects, that leaves five billion of us who are likely to find the idea repulsive.

Sometimes food trends do shift and undesirable foods can become mainstream. This was the case for lobster, once called 'the cockroach of the ocean' and fed to prisoners. But food trends can also fail to gain widespread appeal. Vegetarians have certainly found it hard to convince people to stop eating meat. Trends towards other seemingly unpalatable foods, such as offal meat, in the US have gained a following, but haven't led to large scale change yet.

More interesting is the push to include insects as a part of the farm animal's diet, thus reducing the demand for fishmeal and grains. Although there are areas of the world (including the EU) where insects are currently prohibited as animal feed, this seems a more likely entry point into the food system than trying to change ingrained cultural food preferences.

25 July 2014

⇨ The above information is reprinted with kind permission from Forum for the Future. Please visit www.forumforthefuture.org for further information.

Eating insects: good for you, good for the environment

THE CONVERSATION

An article from The Conversation.

By Susan Lawler, Head of Department, Department of Environmental Management & Ecology at La Trobe University

The Food and Agriculture Organization of the United Nations released a report on Monday called *Edible Insects: Future prospects for food and feed security* and since then news outlets have been looking for images of people eating bugs.

Even I was on our local TV news this week commenting on the issue. The reporter who rang to seek my input asked if I would be willing to eat a live bug for the camera. I politely declined, not just because I am a vegetarian, and not because I am squeamish. As I told the reporter and camera man, if I were to eat an animal, it would most certainly be a bug.

Indeed, I probably eat bugs all the time. As explained by an insect food producer to the ABC, most of us eat a quarter of a kilogram of insects by accident each year. Insects find their way into our foodstuffs no matter how hard we try to keep them out. Interestingly, if you eat organic, your rate of insect consumption is much higher.

So even though I have avoided eating animal flesh (including fish) for over 30 years, I nevertheless engage in entomophagy. And so do billions of people all over the world.

It is not true that the eating of insects is something that humans resort to only when they are starving. Many cultures cherish the flavours and texture of insects. Right here in Australia, indigenous people travelled to the Alps each summer to feast on the bounty provided by the annual influx of bogong moths.

Which, you might say, is fine for them but not likely to convince me to fry up some moths (hint: remove the wings by scorching). So what are the arguments for entomophagy, and why on earth does the United Nations want us to do this apparently disgusting thing?

Eating insects is efficient, good for the environment, improves animal welfare and reduces the risk of diseases in humans. Let's go through the arguments presented in the FAO report.

Efficient feed conversion

The amount of feed you need to provide to get animal-based food varies greatly depending on the species. Predatory fish are expensive to raise in aquaculture because they need to be fed fish. Herbivores are more efficient, but it still takes 10 kilograms of food to produce one kilogram of cow, only half of which can actually be eaten. By contrast, 10 kilograms of feed will produce up to nine kilograms of insects, of which over 95% can be eaten. If we want to find a way to produce more protein with less, insects are the way to go.

Food inputs from waste

Now let's talk about what kind of food we give our livestock. If we have to catch fish to feed our aquaculture fish we are still dependent on wild-caught protein. If we grow grain to feed our cattle, we still have to use land and fertiliser and water. But if we choose to raise insects we can feed them our waste products. Think about it, flies grow on manure. Other insects could grow on agricultural waste products high in cellulose. This transcends efficiency. Growing insects for food could actually clean up the mess made by growing other food.

Less greenhouse gases

Cattle produce so many greenhouse gases that a kilogram of beef has an impact similar to driving 250 kilometres in a car. The only insects that even produce methane as a waste product are cockroaches, termites and scarab beetles. Getting our protein from insects would significantly reduce greenhouse gas emissions.

Water savings

Agriculture consumes 70% of water worldwide, and the production of animal protein requires 100 times more

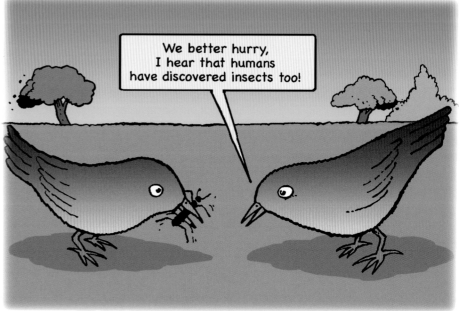

water than protein from grain. This includes the water used to grow the grain to feed the animal, also known as 'virtual water'. By this method of calculation, one kilogram of chicken requires 3,500 litres of water and one kilogram of beef requires between 22,000 and 43,000 litres of water. Insects need far less, and can be grown throughout the drought.

'If we really want people to eat more bugs (and we do!), then I don't think we want to give the impression that we will have to start picking crickets up off the lawn and popping them in our mouths'

Animal welfare

All of our concerns about live animal exports and battery farm hens are based on the need to reduce animal suffering. High density of livestock is necessary for commercial food production but is undesirable from an animal welfare point of view. Insects, on the other hand, are naturally gregarious. Many of them prefer to live in high densities and killing them humanely is possible and easy. No more nightmare film clips from abattoirs.

Reduced risk of disease

Think about the infections that move from animals to people and have frightened all of us: swine flu, bird flu, mad cow disease. These infections are called zoonotics, and they spread because we are similar enough to our livestock to be able to catch their diseases. Insects have a much lower risk of passing disease on to us.

In fact, it is difficult to find many disadvantages to eating insects. We don't even have to get over our aversion to biting into a crunchy morsel with too many legs. Factories are already growing insects to produce protein powders which can be used to supplement foods we already enjoy.

The only downside I could find is that eating fresh insects collected in the wild puts you at risk of consuming pesticides. Which is one of the reasons I did not want to eat a bug for the camera – we did not have any insects from a trusted source.

The other reason is the backlash that could result from the disgust factor. Yes, it would make good TV viewing, because it is shocking and kind of gross. But if we really want people to eat more bugs (and we do!), then I don't think we want to give the impression that we will have to start picking crickets up off the lawn and popping them in our mouths.

No, we are much more sophisticated than that. Insect protein will be produced by reputable growers who will care for their charges and ensure a high-quality product. Make no mistake, this is a growth industry.

In future, entomophagy will be something we do by design, instead of by accident.

16 May 2013

⇨ The above information is reprinted with kind permission from The Conversation. Please visit www.theconversation.com for further information.

Should vegetarians consider eating insects?

By Luke J. Davis

In the last few years, there has been a push from various bodies – including the UN – to get Western countries to adopt eating insects as an alternative to meat. Insects have been hailed as a type of super food. They are rich in protein, environmentally friendly to harvest, sustainable, and, they're already eaten, and enjoyed, in many other parts of the world. There have been a number of occasions recently that I've been asked, as a (moral) vegetarian, for my thoughts on eating insects. 'What if...?' and 'Would you...?' questions are quite a common occurrence for veggies, but this one actually got me thinking.

The immediate response, to me, seems to be: Well, it depends on why the person has decided to become vegetarian. There are three central moral reasons I can think of that could motivate a person's choice to become vegetarian. They are: 1) Reduction of environmental impact; 2) Reduction of suffering; and, 3) A belief that unnecessary killing is wrong. Applied to the case of insects, it seems to me that only (3) provides possible grounds against the practice. But, I'll address all three here.

1) The reduction of environmental impact

A common reason for vegetarianism concerns the fact that meat production causes quite significant environmental damage. As things currently stand, the meat industry is responsible for a non-negligible percentage of annual anthropogenic greenhouse gas emissions (about 14% according to Wikipedia), and is a significant contributor to water pollution. Eating meat supports such bad environmental practices, and thus people choose to refrain on environmental grounds.

Insects don't pose the same problem. The same amount of crop used for beef production can produce nine times the amount of produce in insects. This means that there is significantly less environmental and water costs involved in their production. In fact, one of the central arguments deployed in favour of eating insects is their environmental friendliness and efficiency of production. The environmental argument, then, seems to fail as a reason for not eating insects.

2) The reduction of suffering

Another reason for vegetarianism concerns the infliction of unnecessary suffering. The production and slaughter of huge numbers of animals a year causes suffering that need not occur. There are a sufficient number of alternatives to meat out there that most of us could do without it if we so chose. This isn't the case for everyone, of course. But, it is reasonable (to my mind) to say that eating meat is permissible if one has no other option. Even then suffering should be minimized. However, as I've already said, for most of us meat consumption isn't necessary. This means that the suffering caused by the meat industry is also – in a large part – not necessary. Thus, some choose to abstain from supporting the industry.

This, too, fails as an argument against eating insects. Research does not, on balance, support the view that insects feel pain. The inability to feel pain should assuage most, if not all, of our concerns about suffering. It may be that the ability to feel physical pain is not a necessary condition for the possibility of suffering. However, I imagine that the type of suffering that does not involve physical pain would require rather sophisticated cognitive abilities. I doubt that insects have the necessary cognitive abilities for this form of suffering.[1] Thus, the arguments for vegetarianism that are based on the belief that we have a moral obligation to reduce suffering where we can are insufficient to demonstrate the impermissibility of eating insects.[2] (Even Peter Singer seems to find eating insects permissible.)

3) A belief that unnecessary killing is wrong

A last reason for vegetarianism concerns the belief that it is wrong to raise something merely to kill it, when we don't need to. This isn't like the suffering argument. The concern isn't that the meat industry causes unnecessary pain, but rather that the practice of raising livestock for slaughter is wrong. This means that the meat industry would be impermissible even if all meat were 'happy meat' and

1 The type of suffering I'm thinking of here would be emotional or cognitive (or a mixture of the two). No physical sensation of pain is necessary for either of those, but they certainly count as suffering to my mind.

2 Assuming that current research is correct. If it is not, then the argument will need to be reevaluated. I imagine that the reevaluation would have to take the form of a weighing between the benefits of reduced environmental impact and the losses of inflicting suffering. The balance that is struck between these two will depend on empirical factors such as the amount of insect production and the extent to which it displaces current meat production.

produced in an environmentally sustainable way. People who take this view are vegetarian because they view the practice of eating meat itself as wrong.

This could motivate an argument against eating insects: Insects are living things. Raising living things to kill them is wrong. Thus, we shouldn't raise and kill insects. Now I have to admit that I find this argument compelling when applied to animals we more typically associate with the meat industry. Animals that are more cognitively sophisticated than insects, and – if I'm being honest – that I can empathize with. Empathy is important because it signals to me that these other animals can have an interest that is worth protecting. In this case it's the interest in not being slaughtered. When such an interest is present, we have an obligation to take it into consideration. The interest in staying alive is a very strong one indeed, stronger than our interest in eating meat (again, for those of us for whom it is a choice). Thus, we ought to refrain from raising animals to kill them.

Can the same be said of insects? I doubt it. For the same reason they don't qualify as candidates for cognitive or emotional suffering, I doubt they qualify as bearers of a sufficiently strong interest. It seems, then, that the third argument also fails to provide grounds against eating insects. I'm still uneasy about the idea, but can't summon any principled grounds why. Maybe, then, those who are vegetarian for one or all of the three reasons mentioned above shouldn't have a problem with eating insects. I'd be interested to know what others think.

24 June 2014

⇨ The above information is reprinted with kind permission from Practical Ethics. Please visit blog.practicalethics.ox.ac. uk for further information.

Healthy diet could reduce greenhouse gases and extend life expectancy, research shows

A healthy diet, which consists of fruit, veg and cereals – alongside less meat and savoury snacks – could reduce greenhouse gases by nearly a fifth, according to research.

It could also reduce the risk of health problems such as heart disease, stroke and type 2 diabetes, and could even extend average life expectancy by eight months.

Scientists at the London School of Hygiene & Tropical Medicine said eating better would benefit both people's health and the environment.

The diets of the average UK man and woman do not currently conform to World Health Organization (WHO) recommendations but its study suggested that if they did, greenhouse gas emissions would be reduced by 17%.

Researchers analysed food diaries from more than 1,500 adults in the UK and looked at how diet affected health problems such as coronary heart disease, stroke, type 2 diabetes and a number of cancers.

They said diet-related ill health in the UK is estimated to cost the NHS around £6 billion annually, but calculated that eating more healthily could save almost seven million years of life lost prematurely in the UK over the next 30 years.

They estimated that it would also extend average life expectancy by around eight months (12 months for men and four months for women).

These health gains would come mainly from reductions in coronary heart disease and stroke, they said.

'Encouraging people in the UK to modify their diets to contain fewer animal products and processed foods and more cereals, fruit and vegetables would produce tangible benefits to both health and the environment,' researchers said.

But they added that the health benefits and acceptability of such diets is likely to peak at around a 40% reduction in greenhouse gas emissions as greater reductions than this would be likely to result in 'unacceptable diets and progressively reduced health gains' – although these would still be an improvement on current diets.

They said 'radical' dietary changes such as veganism were not necessary in order for there to be large reductions in emissions and benefits to health.

One of the authors, Dr Alan Dangour, said: 'This is the most detailed analysis to date for the UK and our findings show that even making relatively small changes to current diets would have a tremendous impact on both the environment and population health.

'It's clear from our analysis that we do not need to make radical changes to our dietary habits to bring about substantial benefits.

'We hope the detailed information we've compiled about the composition of healthy and low-emission diets will help to prioritise policies and interventions aimed at promoting healthier and more environmentally-sustainable diets.'

1 May 2015

⇨ The above information is reprinted with kind permission from The Huffington Post UK. Please visit www. huffingtonpost.co.uk for further information.

Alternative diets: can a radical food regime help fight illness?

Desperate to alleviate the debilitating symptoms caused by Crohn's disease, diabetes, back pain and autism, three women and one family all found relief through radical diets.

By Amy Bryant

Ruth Twort, 49, lives in London with her husband, Andrew, and their daughter, Hannah

When Ruth Twort was told she had Crohn's disease at the age of 19, it was the first time she'd heard of it. 'I was 17 when I started to faint at school. I'd get stabbing pains in my abdomen, and would be sick, rushing to the lavatory with loose stools. It affected my confidence terribly.' She started to cut out foods. 'I thought, "Maybe it's wheat, maybe milk." When I heard I had Crohn's, an inflammation of the intestines, I learnt I wasn't absorbing nutrients from food.' After an operation to remove a section of her intestine for biopsy – 'the doctor did a motion with his hands, it was an arm's length' – Ruth was given steroids. 'It was like putting a plaster on a serious disease. I wanted to learn how to heal my gut, but when I discussed diet with my doctors they were like, "Forget it." '

Instead, she attended a course at the Institute for Optimum Nutrition, in London. 'I tried the Hay Diet, the raw food diet, every theory I could find on Crohn's disease, but I couldn't put my finger on the results. Every time I had a flare-up – stomach pain, swollen ankles – I never knew if what I was eating was causing me harm.' For ten years Ruth was on and off steroids, surviving on supplements and friendly bacteria powders. Then she discovered *Controlling Crohn's Disease: The Natural Way*, by Virginia Harper. It described Harper's battle with Crohn's – 'She was told, as I had been, "Here's a disability badge, you're not going to be able to work, you won't have children"– and her solution: a macrobiotic lifestyle. It was my eureka moment.' The regime Harper expounded – nutrient-dense miso soup and vegetables for breakfast, brown rice and soaked wakame for lunch – was easier to adopt after a macrobiotic cookery class. 'I incorporated the meals into dinner parties,' says Ruth. 'Even my husband, a meat-and-cheese man, took to them.'

When Ruth's health deteriorated again in her mid-30s and a major blood clot was discovered in her leg, consultants claimed it stemmed from Crohn's. 'They said I was making things difficult for myself by refusing steroids and continuing to eat miso soup in hospital.' A second investigation revealed that a rupture in the original operation on Ruth's intestine had led to the clot: 'If I hadn't been doing the macrobiotics, I wouldn't have been alive.'

Today, Ruth follows a 60 per cent macrobiotic diet, eating whole foods done in a pressure cooker to aid digestion. 'Salads are useless because I can't absorb them; instead, I chop up carrots, celery and broccoli.' She was 41 when her daughter, Hannah, was born. Ruth hasn't been to a doctor for ten years, and now advises others with fertility problems. 'From being the worst case doctors had seen, I've not had a single twinge since. It's been a triumph.'

The macrobiotic diet

⇨ Rooted in traditional Eastern philosophy of yin and yang, whereby opposite energies should be balanced for better health and well-being

⇨ Mainly vegetarian, the diet is based on natural, unprocessed foods: whole grains (soaked overnight); millet mash

⇨ Dairy, sugar and red meat are avoided, beans, vegetables and seaweed (iodine-rich) encouraged

⇨ Foods are largely steamed or blanched instead of pan-fried, juiced or eaten raw

⇨ Promotes digestive and thyroid health, higher energy levels, better-looking skin.

Michael, 39, and Helen Lee, 40, have two children and live in Whitby

It was a chance link on YouTube that led to Michael and Helen Lee adopting the GAPS diet with their 11-year-old daughter, Olivia, last summer. Olivia was seven-and-a-half when she was diagnosed with non-verbal autism, and, despite receiving excellent support from her school, her family had little help from doctors or therapists. 'They said there was nothing they could do for her,' recalls Helen. 'Anything we did to try to help Olivia, we found out on the Internet or from other parents.'

Around Easter last year, Olivia's symptoms worsened. Michael says, 'Her behaviour was deteriorating. We were trying to arrange more respite care, but she screamed every time we left the room.' Helen adds, 'She would nip and scratch us, go for her brother Jacob or make herself vomit. She was raging – there's no other word for it.'

Desperate, Michael searched online and found some interviews with Dr Natasha Campbell-McBride, the author of *Gut and Psychology Syndrome* (or GAPS). 'We watched with chins on the floor, thinking, "She's just described everything we've been through in the past ten years." They immediately ordered the book. 'I read it four times over our holiday,' says Michael.

In it, Campbell-McBride, the mother of an autistic son, describes how the digestive system affects the brain. Helen uses the analogy of a leaky pipe: 'Olivia's digestive system doesn't work as it should and leaks poison into her blood, affecting the clarity of her brain.'

'The idea behind the GAPS protocol,' Michael continues, 'is to avoid anything unnatural getting into her bloodstream. Everything she eats should be made from scratch.'

The Lees embarked on the introduction diet in full earlier this year, under the guidance of Sarah Hanratty, a nutritionist and GAPS practitioner. 'We did it as a family, so that Olivia wouldn't feel alienated. We make soups with stocks cooked from scratch, and home-baked crackers have replaced bread. We cut out ingredients that could potentially cause Olivia harm, then gradually reintroduce them, keeping watch for any change in her symptoms. She's eating fruit again, cooked in ways that are easier on her digestive system, and we are just considering whether to add dairy back in. It's not a quick fix.'

But, much to her parents' delight, Olivia is already showing signs of improvement. 'She's sleeping so much better. Her learning has come on in leaps and bounds, and she's no longer doubly incontinent.' Best of all, Helen concludes, 'She's smiling and laughing again. Autism is like a fog that stops you seeing clearly, and this diet has helped that fog to lift.

'It's not a cure, but it's helping to make Olivia more comfortable. We've got our little girl back.'

The GAPS diet

⇨ Treats the gut to detoxify the bloodstream and improve mental development in children with autism, ADHD, dyspraxia or dyslexia

⇨ Foods with grains, sugar and starchy vegetables are replaced with dishes made with ground nuts, natural honey and dried fruit

⇨ The diet begins with home-made stocks and broths, then soups and probiotic home-made yogurt. Casseroles, raw veg, and pancakes are then introduced.

Julie Cove, 50, lives in British Columbia, with her husband and three children

An alkaline diet finally brought relief to Julie Cove, an interior designer, after almost two years of debilitating back and leg pain caused by a herniated disc. 'When my youngest daughter was one I started getting stabbing pains in my back. The pain shot down my left leg and I lost feeling in my toes. I was pretty much flat on my back for four months.' Cue visits to chiropractors and physiotherapists, then sessions of acupuncture, laser light therapy and water therapy. 'Nothing changed. I was immobile and in serious pain.' A neurosurgeon who recommended back surgery warned that she'd never be able to pick up her daughter again. 'I left,' Julie says, 'bawling.'

Julie resorted to microscopic surgery to reduce the fluid within the disc: 'I needed my life back. I couldn't run my business, drive my kids to school or be part of my family.' She was up and walking by the end of the day but, two months later, the pain returned. A chance meeting with an old acquaintance gave Julie hope. 'She was a painter who, having breathed in toxic paint chemicals for 20 years, developed arthritis to the worst degree. She told me to see these alkaline consultants, two sisters, saying, "They've changed my world." I called them that day.'

Julie's weekly check-ups started with a live blood analysis, showing her blood cells under a microscope. 'They were misshapen, with high levels of acidity. I learnt I needed to up my alkaline intake, eating food with an alkalising effect. I finally realised I could heal myself from the inside-out.'

Starting the alkaline diet was like going 'cold turkey'. Julie's sister, Yvonne, joined her, and they began drinking only vegetable juices and water for three days. 'Next, we could make soups. Then we could eat only vegetables for six weeks. When fish was introduced, I thought we'd gone to heaven.' Alkaline water and nutritional supplements were also part of the diet, and the sisters referred to Dr Robert Young's *The pH Miracle*, which lists foods' alkalising effects. Julie was pain-free in three months, having reduced the inflammation enough to stop the disc touching the nerve. She has since sold her business, studied to be a nutritionist and started a blog, sharing her experience and recipes. Her book is due out in 2015. 'It feels so good to know I have so many healthy years ahead of me.'

The alkaline lifestyle

⇨ Most foods, when fully digested, will break down into either an acid or alkaline base

⇨ Wheat, dairy, meat and fish have an acidic effect and are largely avoided. Nuts, legumes, greens and some fruits are alkaline

⇨ A daily ratio of 80 per cent alkaline foods to 20 per cent acid foods is encouraged to balance the body's pH

⇨ Muscle pain, stress, headaches and heart disease can all be helped on this diet.

Wendy Yaxley, 48, lives in Lincoln with her husband, Peter. They have four children

'I wouldn't be surprised if you were dead by the time you're 50.' It was with those words ringing in her ears that Wendy Yaxley left her doctor's surgery in 2009, having been diagnosed with type 2 diabetes. 'I weighed nearly 19 stone. One of my legs had been badly damaged by deep vein thrombosis years before and they told me I would lose it if it started to ulcerate. I was devastated.'

Wendy had dieted all her life but could only lose a few pounds. 'I was eating all the recommended diet foods and went for long walks every day. My meal sizes became incredibly small. I couldn't understand why nothing was changing.' At 18st 11lb in her mid-30s, she sought medical help. 'I had blurred vision. I had to stop driving.' When a thyroid test came back normal, 'My doctor wrote me a prescription for antidepressants but I gave it back. I didn't want to be treated for depression; I wanted to know what was wrong with me.'

Wendy's daughter, Jade, pleaded with her to try a diet that focused on foods that appear low down on the glycaemic index. 'I told her I couldn't cope with diets any more, but she insisted.' After a month following recipes aimed specifically at diabetics, Wendy lost a stone. Desperate to read more, she found Patrick Holford's *Low-GL Diet Bible*. 'I cried all through it. I felt he'd written it just for me. He explained why diet foods didn't work, why I'd stayed fat and struggled to lose weight. I suddenly realised there might be a way out of diabetes.'

The book, well thumbed and annotated, remains in Wendy's kitchen. 'Every day is a low-GL day,' she says. 'I start with porridge oats and stir in ground pumpkin seeds or grated apple. I measure my carbohydrates (45g brown basmati rice with a home-made beef and vegetable curry, for example), and I've learnt to chew food properly.'

Within a week of following the full Holford diet, Wendy's sight had improved and her joints no longer ached. Now 12st 12lb, her BMI has dropped from 46 to 29. 'Most importantly, my blood sugars have returned to normal. When my GP said he was taking me off the diabetic register, I had to ask him to say it twice! He couldn't believe it either. I hope to be around to see my grandchildren grow up.'

The low-GI diet

⇨ GL, or glycaemic load, measures carbohydrate in food and the effect it will have on blood sugar

⇨ Foods with a low GL score (under ten) have little impact (rye bread, blackberries, broccoli). High-GL foods (over 20), could cause a sharp rise in glucose (bagels, raisins, baked potato)

⇨ Aim to eat no more than 45 GLs a day. Low-GL carbs are OK. Sugar, saturated fats, caffeine and alcohol are not

⇨ Can help tiredness, skin and lower risk of diabetes, heart disease, cancer and arthritis.

6 December 2013

⇨ The above information is reprinted with kind permission from *The Telegraph*. Please visit www.telegraph.co.uk for further information.

Vegetarian diet 'could have slight benefits in diabetes'

'Vegetable diet will beat diabetes: Meat-free lifestyle cures killer disease,' is the typically overblown headline in the *Daily Express*.

But researchers actually found a vegetarian diet led to a quite modest fall in only one measure of blood glucose called HbA1C, a measure of blood glucose control.

The paper reports on a systematic review which combined the results of six trials that involved 255 people with type 2 diabetes. They examined whether vegetarian or vegan diets improved blood glucose control compared with a control diet.

Overall, the pooled results of five of these trials found a vegetarian or vegan diet reduced HbA1c by 0.39%. There was no significant effect on fasting glucose levels, an assessment of how efficiently the body can process glucose in the short term.

This slight reduction in HbA1c is no cure. As the researchers themselves pointed out, the reduction is less than you would expect if a patient was being treated with the drug of choice for type 2 diabetes, metformin.

This review also has various important limitations, including the variable design and quality of the six trials included. So, it does not prove that a vegetarian or vegan diet is better for a person with type 2 diabetes, and any media claims of a 'cure' for the condition are entirely baseless.

Where did the story come from?

The study was carried out by researchers from Keio University in Japan and The George Washington University School of Medicine in the US.

Funding was provided by the Japan Society for the Promotion of Science and the Nestlé Nutrition Council, Japan.

One of the co-authors declared a non-financial conflict of interest. This author serves as president of the Physicians Committee for Responsible Medicine, without financial compensation.

This organisation is described in the publication as one that, 'promotes the use of low-fat, plant-based diets and discourages the use of animal-derived, fatty and sugary foods'. This represents a potential conflict of interest in the interpretation of the results.

The study was published in the peer-reviewed medical journal, *Cardiovascular Diagnosis and Therapy* and the study is open access, so it is free to read the study online.

The *Daily Express*' coverage of the study is accurate and contains some useful background information, so it is frustrating that its headline is totally misleading, especially as it was on the front page.

In fact, this review of studies found vegetarian or vegan diets caused a slight reduction in HbA1c compared with non-vegetarian diets. This is not a cure in any sense of the word.

The current thinking is that there is no such thing as a cure for type 2 diabetes. The condition can be successfully managed, but not cured.

The study is also only applicable to type 2 diabetes, so the headlines do not apply to type 1 diabetes.

What kind of research was this?

This was a systematic review and meta-analysis combining the results of controlled trials that examined the effects of vegetarian diets on blood sugar control in type 2 diabetes.

As the researchers say, previous research has suggested a link between a vegetarian diet and improved blood sugar control, but the relationship is not well established.

As an interesting aside, the researchers highlight how diabetes levels were found to be lower in Seventh-day Adventists, a Protestant Christian denomination whose followers are encouraged to adopt a vegetarian diet.

This review aimed to examine this grey area. A systematic review and meta-analysis of randomised controlled trials is the best way of examining the evidence to date that has assessed this question.

What did the research involve?

The researchers searched a number of literature databases (from their inception to 2013) to identify published clinical trials examining the effects of a vegetarian, vegan or omnivorous diet on blood sugar control in people with type 2 diabetes who were over the age of 20.

A vegetarian diet was defined as one excluding meat, poultry and fish, while a vegan diet excluded all animal products.

Eligible trials had an intervention duration of at least four weeks and examined the main outcome of changes in HbA1c.

This gives an indication of blood sugar control in the longer term, as it indicates the amount of sugar being carried by red blood cells, which have a lifespan of around three months. Change in fasting blood sugar measures was a secondary outcome.

In an added effort to find all relevant information for the review, the research team scoured the reference lists of all articles they found from the search of electronic databases, and also contacted research experts for additional material.

The researchers assessed the quality of the studies included, and pooled studies calculating the average difference in HbA1c and fasting blood sugar between vegetarian or vegan and comparison diets.

What were the basic results?

A total of six trials met the inclusion criteria, involving 255 people with type 2 diabetes with an average age of 52-and-a-half. The average trial duration was 23.7 weeks, or about six months.

Five of the studies examined vegan diets and one studied vegetarian diets. Four trials were conducted in the US, one in Brazil and one in the Czech Republic.

Of the six studies, three were randomised controlled trials, one was a cluster randomised controlled trial, and two were non-randomised controlled trials.

In the pooled analysis of five trials, the vegetarian or vegan diet was associated with a significant reduction in HbA1c (-0.39%, 95% confidence interval [CI] -0.62 to -0.15) compared with omnivorous control diets.

But the pooled analysis of four trials did not find a statistically significant reduction in fasting blood sugar: the average difference with the vegetarian or vegan diet compared with control was -0.36 mmol/L, 95% CI -1.04 to 0.32.

Compared with control, the vegetarian or vegan diets were also associated with significant reductions in the amount of total energy the diet provided, either through carbohydrate, protein, total fat, cholesterol and fibre.

How did the researchers interpret the results?

The researchers concluded that, 'Consumption of vegetarian diets is associated with improved [blood glucose] control in type 2 diabetes.'

Conclusion

This systematic review has identified six trials assessing whether vegetarian or vegan diets improve blood sugar control in type 2 diabetes compared with control.

It found the vegetarian or vegan diet gave significant improvement in one measure of blood sugar control (HbA1c), but not in another (fasting blood glucose).

However, there are some important limitations to consider before we can categorically conclude that people with type 2 diabetes should switch to a meat and fish-free diet:

The improvement in blood sugar control was quite small

The pooled results of five trials found a vegetarian or vegan diet was associated with a 0.39% reduction in HbA1c, but we don't know that this

would have made any meaningful clinical difference in diabetes control for the individual.

Overall, although any reduction is likely to be a good thing, the precise benefit would depend on what a person's HbA1c level was to start with.

The target HbA1c is usually set at a level below around 7%, so it may be more useful knowing whether a vegetarian or vegan diet improved the proportion of people achieving their target HbA1c level. The review also found no improvement in fasting blood glucose control.

The intervention diets were varied

Despite the publication tending to refer to the intervention diets as vegetarian, they were actually quite varied across the trials.

Four of the trials were described as low-fat vegan, one as lacto-vegetarian (a diet that includes dairy products but not eggs), and one lacto-ovo low-protein (similar to a lacto-vegetarian diet but, as the name suggests, with a focus on low-protein foods).

The control diets were also quite varied across the trials

The researchers included diets described as omnivorous, low fat, 'diabetic diet' and those that followed American Diabetic Association guidance.

Overall, this doesn't give a very clear picture of what diets were being compared, which makes it hard to conclude that a particular diet is associated with an improvement in blood sugar control compared with a particular control.

The trials had variable quality evidence

Only three of the six trials studied were true randomised controlled trials. They varied in the duration of the dietary intervention between four and 74 weeks.

Also, only one of the six trials (a controlled trial) is reported to have made any adjustment for potential confounders (sex, baseline HbA1c level and medication). The others report no adjustment.

We also don't know how the trials checked that the diets were being followed as assigned, or of any

other intervention or advice that may have been given to the participants alongside the dietary intervention (such as advice about physical activity).

The review only included published trials

In their assessment of possible publication bias, the researchers observed that smaller trials that found reductions in HbA1c level were perhaps more likely to have been published and therefore included in this review.

The small number of participants

Despite this being a systematic review of trials, the total number of participants was still quite small, at only 255. This is a very small number of patients, and it might be unwise to base any firm or generalisable conclusions on such small numbers.

A vegetarian or vegan diet can be a healthy lifestyle choice for a person with type 2 diabetes if it provides balanced nutrition. But such diets can still be high in fat, salt and sugar if this is not controlled carefully.

A healthy diet needs to be combined with regular exercise for people to be able to reap further health benefits, as well as avoiding smoking and only consuming alcohol at or below nationally recommended levels.

Overall, this review does not appear to conclusively prove that a vegetarian or vegan diet is better for a person with type 2 diabetes. It certainly provides no evidence that this diet cures diabetes, as one of the news headlines suggests.

Provided you do your homework, it is possible to eat healthily on a vegetarian or vegan diet. But if you do have type 2 diabetes, we recommend that you talk to the doctor in charge of your care before making any radical changes to your diet.

24 November 2014

⇨ The above information is reprinted with kind permission from NHS Choices. Please visit www.nhs.uk for further information.

Diet swap has dramatic effects on colon cancer risk for Americans and Africans

By Sam Wong

Scientists have found dramatic effects on risk factors for colon cancer when American and African volunteers swapped diets for just two weeks.

Western diets, high in protein and fat but low in fibre, are thought to raise colon cancer risk compared with African diets high in fibre and low in fat and protein.

The new study, published in *Nature Communications* today, confirms that a high fibre diet can substantially reduce risk, and shows that bacteria living in the gut play an important role in this effect.

Colon cancer is the fourth commonest cause of death from cancer worldwide, accounting for over 600,000 deaths per year. Colon cancer rates are much higher in the western world than in Africa or the Far East, yet in the United States, African Americans shoulder the greatest burden of the disease.

To investigate the possible roles of diet and gut bacteria, an international team including scientists from the University of Pittsburgh and Imperial College London carried out a study with a group of 20 African American volunteers and another group of 20 participants from rural South Africa. The two groups swapped diets under tightly controlled conditions for two weeks.

The volunteers had colonoscopy examinations before and after the diet swap. The researchers also measured biological markers that indicate colon cancer risk and studied samples of bacteria taken from the colon.

At the start, when the groups had been eating their normal diets, almost half of the American subjects had polyps – abnormal growths in the bowel lining that may be harmless but can progress to cancer. None of the Africans had these abnormalities.

After two weeks on the African diet, the American group had significantly less inflammation in the colon and reduced biomarkers of cancer risk. In the African group, measurements indicating cancer risk dramatically increased after two weeks on the western diet.

Professor Jeremy Nicholson, the team leader from the Department of Surgery and Cancer at Imperial College London, said: 'We can't definitively tell from these measurements that the change in their diet would have led to more cancer in the African group or less in the American group, but there is good evidence from other studies that the changes we observed are signs of cancer risk.

'The findings suggest that people can substantially lower their risk of colon cancer by eating more fibre. This is not new in itself but what is really surprising is how quickly and dramatically the risk markers can switch in both groups following diet change. These findings also raise serious concerns that the progressive westernisation of African communities may lead to the emergence of colon cancer as a major health issue.'

Professor Stephen O'Keefe at the University of Pittsburgh, who directed the study, said: 'Studies on Japanese migrants to Hawaii have shown that it takes one generation of westernisation to change their low incidence of colon cancer to the high rates observed in native Hawaiians. Our study suggests that westernisation of the diet induces changes in biomarkers of colon cancer risk in the colonic mucosa within two weeks. Perhaps even more importantly, a change in diet from a westernised composition to a "traditional African" high fibre low fat diet reduced these biomarkers of cancer risk within two weeks, indicating that it is likely never too late to change your diet to change your risk of colon cancer.'

The study found that a major reason for the changes in cancer risk was the way in which the bacteria in the gut – known as the microbiome – altered their metabolism to adapt to the new diet. In the American group, the researchers found that the African diet led to an increase in the production of butyrate, a byproduct of fibre metabolism that has important anti-cancer effects.

Dr James Kinross, a colorectal surgeon and a member of the research group at Imperial, said: 'The gut microbiome is being increasingly recognized as an important contributor to human health. This research shows that gut bacteria are critically important for mediating the link between diet and colon cancer risk. This means we can look to develop therapies targeting gut bacteria as a way to prevent and treat cancer.'

The study was funded by the National Institutes of Health in the US and the National Institute for Health Research Imperial Biomedical Research Centre in the UK.

Reference: S.J.D. O'Keefe et al. 'Fat, fibre and cancer risk in African Americans and rural Africans.' *Nature Communications*, 2015. DOI: 10.1038/ncomms7342

28 April 2015

⇨ The above information is reprinted with kind permission from Imperial College London. Please visit www.imperial.ac.uk for further information.

Key facts

- There are currently huge pressures on the global food system. The demand for food is increasing with the growing global population (which is expected to increase from seven billion today to over nine billion by 2050) and also with the increase in wealth in emerging economies. (page 1)

- Over one billion people worldwide are overweight or obese. (page 1)

- One billion others do not have access to adequate food. (page 1)

- An additional one billion have inadequate micronutrient intakes (page 1)

- The global population will increase from nearly seven billion today to eight billion by 2030, and to probably over nine billion by 2050. Historically the global population growth rate was very low and prior to the industrial revolution (from the 18th to the 19th century) the world's population was less than one billion people. (page 2)

- The global food system currently uses 70% of the extracted fresh water and 34.3% of the land area, and is a major producer of greenhouse gas (GHG) emissions. (page 2)

- Globally, agriculture (including fertiliser production) directly contributes ten to 12% of GHG emissions. This figure rises to 30% or more when land conversion and costs beyond the farm gate are added. (page 2)

- In the UK, GHG emissions associated with agriculture are lower than the global average at approximately 7%, as are total GHG emissions associated with the food supply chain (i.e. production and consumption) at approximately 18%. (page 2)

- UK farming and fishing account for about one third of GHG emissions from the food supply chain (approximately 7% of the total). The majority of GHG emissions are due to emissions from ruminant animals (i.e. cows and sheep) and the oxidisation of nitrogen in fertilisers. (page 2)

- Net trade and commercial transportation contribute 25% and 9% respectively of the GHG emissions in the UK food chain (net trade covers emissions related to the production of food imports and exports, but not transportation). (page 2)

- Today in Britain, the vegetarian diet is firmly on the map with 12% of UK adults following a vegetarian or vegan diet, rising to 20% of 16 to 24s. (page 7)

- Today, as many as one in eight (13%) UK meat-buyers claim they would be interested in buying half and half products from the supermarket, with 50% red meat and 50% vegetable protein for example. (page 7)

- Greenhouse gas emissions for a meat-based diet are approximately twice as high as those for vegans, and about 50 per cent higher than for vegetarians. (page 11)

- Meat is a good source of protein, vitamins and minerals in your diet. However, the Department of Health has advised that people who eat a lot of red and processed meat a day (more than 90g cooked weight) cut down to 70g. (page 13)

- Around 1.3 billion people worldwide live from animal husbandry – most of them in developing countries. (page 17)

- The European Union offers subsidies for fodder crops and supports up to 40 per cent of the cost of investing in new animal housing. (page 17)

- There will be an estimated extra two billion people globally by 2050, meaning the food system will need to feed over nine billion people. The UN Food and Agricultural Organisation (FAO) estimates that this will require overall food production to increase by about 70% by 2050, with an extra 200 million tonnes of meat produced to meet the growing demand. (page 19)

- Less than two per cent of the population has a food allergy, but millions more believe they suffer from the condition and they are proving to be a lucrative market for manufacturers. (page 25)

- According to the Food Standards Agency, the British gluten-free market is worth £238 million annually and grew by more than 15 per cent last year. (page 25)

- One kilogram of chicken requires 3,500 litres of water and one kilogram of beef requires between 22,000 and 43,000 litres of water. (page 32)

Flexitarian

Sometimes known as "semi" or "demi" vegetarian. A term coined to describe a diet which is mostly vegetarian but occasionally includes meat consumption, although this is often limited to only fish or white meat.

Free-range

Meat and eggs which have been sourced from animals raised in an outdoor environment with the freedom to roam around. The European Union stipulates the standards to which farmers have to adhere in order to label their produce as free-range.

Intensive farming

Intensive farming involves high levels of input (labour and cost) in order to maximise output of a product. In livestock farming, this can mean large numbers of animals cramped into a very limited space. This is sometimes called factory farming, and has been criticised for its disregard for the welfare of animals.

Low-GI Diet

A low-glycemic diet focuses on foods that have a low glycemic index (GI). This keeps blood sugar levels stable and helps us metabolise fat.

Macrobiotic Diet

A dietary regime that avoids processed and refined foods, focussing instead on grains and vegetables.

Meat substitute

Also referred to as meat analogues, meat substitutes imitate the texture and quality of meat but are made from non-animal products such as soya, tofu, mycoprotein or similar. Meat substitutes are popular with some vegetarians as sources of fibre and protein: others, however, dislike the taste and texture of anything resembling meat.

Meat-Free Monday

A campaign launched by Sir Paul McCartney which encourages people to have at least one meat-free day per week. The main reason behind the campaign is to reduce to the effect of meat consumption on the environment.

Omega-3

A polyunsaturated fatty acid commonly found in oily fish (such as salmon) and some nuts (such as walnuts), omega-3 is thought to reduce the risk of heart disease and aid the development of the brain.

Organic

Food which has been produced without the use of chemical fertilisers or pesticides. It takes many years for soil to become truly organic and free from any man-made chemicals. Organic food must meet certain legal standards before it can legitimately be called "organic".

Orthorexia nervosa

An eating disorder and mental health condition characterised by an extreme avoidance of food that the sufferer considers to be unhealthy.

Paleo Diet

A diet that is based on the principle of only consuming foods that were available to early human-beings. This includes meat, fish certain vegetables and fruit – but excludes products such as dairy and any processed foods.

Pescatarian

A term sometimes used to describe someone who excludes all meat from their diet with the exception of fish. Some people who eat fish and no other meat choose to refer to themselves as vegetarians, however, because the term "pescatarian" is not widely used or understood. However, eating fish means they do not follow a 100% vegetarian diet.

Protein

Proteins are chains of amino acids that allow the body to build and repair body tissue. Protein is found in dairy foods, meat, fish and soya beans.

Quorn

Quorn is the well-known brand name of a large vegetarian food range. Quorn products are made from a type of fungi called mycoprotein.

Soya

A bushy herb native to Asia. The seed from the soybean plant is an excellent source of protein and is often used as a meat substitute.

Sustainable diet

Sustainable diets have a low environmental impact – this includes the impact of food production and consumption on our planet's resources.

Vegan

Someone who does not eat any animal products at all; they exclude meat, fish, poultry, dairy products, eggs and honey from their diet (any food deriving from an animal source).

Vegetarian

Someone who does not eat meat, fish, poultry or any slaughterhouse by-product such as gelatine. There are different types of vegetarian, including lacto-ovo vegetarians, who eat both eggs and dairy; ovo vegetarians, who eat eggs but not dairy; and lacto vegetarians, who eat dairy but not eggs.

Assignments

Brainstorming

⇨ In small groups, discuss what you know about alternative diets. Consider the following:

- What is meant by the term 'sustainable diet'?

- What are some of the alternative diets you have heard of?

- What is the difference between vegetarianism and veganism?

Research

⇨ Choose one of the alternative diets mentioned in this book and conduct further research into what foods are encouraged/discouraged on your chosen regime. Summarise your findings in bullet-point form and compare with a class-mate who researched a different diet.

⇨ Conduct a survey amongst your friends, family and class-mates to investigate how much meat they eat on a daily basis. Write a summary of your findings and include graphs and tables.

⇨ Research the Paleo Diet and write two columns of bullet points that detail arguments for and against the diet.

⇨ There is an ongoing debate over whether a vegetarian diet is more or less healthy than a diet which includes meat. Carry out your own research into this issue using the articles which look at Vegetarian Nutrition, as well as other sources. Write a brief summary of your findings, outlining each argument and providing your own conclusion.

Design

⇨ Design a poster that could be displayed in your local GP surgery to demonstrate some of the dietary changes that can have a positive impact on diabetes.

⇨ Choose one of the articles from this book and create an illustration that depicts the key themes/messages from that article.

⇨ Create a campaign that will persuade people in the UK to eat less meat. This could be a poster campaign or something social-media based. Think of a name for your campaign and include a logo and tag-line.

⇨ Design your own brand of insect-based snacks. Consider the following:

- key ingredient

- sweet or savoury?

- what form will your snack take? (crisps, sweets, snack-bar, etc.)

- brand name

- advertising material (posters, website, etc.)

Oral

⇨ In pairs, role play a situation in which one of you is a vegetarian trying to persuade your carnivorous friend to eat less meat.

⇨ In small groups, discuss some of the stereotypes that surround vegetarians and vegans. Consider whether you think there is a stigma surrounding male vegetarians.

⇨ 'Gluten-free diets have no real health benefit, they're just a fad.' Debate this motion as a class.

⇨ In pairs, discuss whether you think vegetarians should consider eating insects.

⇨ Create a PowerPoint presentation that explains the importance of sustainable diets.

Reading/writing

⇨ Read the article *Healthy, sustainable diets – what are the issues?* on page one and write a summary of the key issues for your school newspaper.

⇨ Write a one-paragraph definition of flexitarianism.

⇨ Choose one of your favourite recipes, where meat is a key ingredient, and create a vegetarian alternative. Cook the recipe for a friend or family member and write a blog post exploring your success or failure!

⇨ Write an essay exploring the link between eating meat and climate change.

⇨ Choose one of the celebrity diets from the article on pages 21 and 22, and write an article exploring its potential dangers.

⇨ Definitions of what a vegetarian diet should include tend to vary: for example, some people describe themselves as vegetarian and yet eat fish. Write a short summary defining what being a vegetarian means to you. Do you think it is important to establish an accepted definition of vegetarianism, or are we free to choose our own labels?

Acknowledgements

The publisher is grateful for permission to reproduce the material in this book. While every care has been taken to trace and acknowledge copyright, the publisher tenders its apology for any accidental infringement or where copyright has proved untraceable. The publisher would be pleased to come to a suitable arrangement in any such case with the rightful owner.

Images

All images courtesy of iStock, except page 4: Unsplash, page 22 © Monstruo Estrudio and page 29 © Alpha.

Icons on pages 15 and 17 courtesy of Flaticon.

Illustrations

Don Hatcher: pages 12 & 30. Simon Kneebone: pages 3 & 24. Angelo Madrid: pages 20 & 36.

Additional acknowledgements

Editorial on behalf of Independence Educational Publishers by Cara Acred.

With thanks to the Independence team: Mary Chapman, Sandra Dennis, Christina Hughes, Jackie Staines and Jan Sunderland.

Cara Acred

Cambridge

September 2015